Risk-Shaped Discipleship

On Going Deeper into the Life of God

TERRY BIDDINGTON

RESOURCE PUBLICATIONS, INC.
San Jose, California
rpinet.com

Reprint Department
Resource Publications, Inc.
160 E. Virginia Street, Suite #290
San Jose, CA 95112-5876
(408) 286-8505
(408) 287-8748 fax
editor@rpinet.com

Library of Congress Cataloging-in-Publication Data

Biddington, Terry, 1956-
  Risk-shaped discipleship : on going deeper into the life of God / Terry Biddington.
    p. cm.
  Includes bibliographical references.
  ISBN-13: 978-0-89390-693-1 (pbk.)
  ISBN-10: 0-89390-693-X (pbk.)
  1. Christian life. 2. Spirituality. I. Title.
  BV4501.3.B486 2010
  248.4--dc22
                                                2010024794
Printed in the United States of America

10 11 12 13 14 | 5 4 3 2 1

Design and production: Kenneth Guentert, The Publishing Pro, LLC
Copyeditor: Kathi Scarpace
Front cover photo: Fiona Biddington

This book is dedicated gratefully
to the memory of John L. R. Presswell,
priest.

Contents

Acknowledgments

I am delighted to make acknowledgment of the help, encouragement, and critical conversation as this book has come to birth.

To Una Kroll, who lovingly encouraged me to take the plunge and step outside my own comfort zone. To Laura Betson, Nathan Eddy, Chris Jenkins, Bruce Lamb, Clive Larsen, Stephen Lowe, Hilary Topp, William West, and Eric Biddington, kinsman and inspirational composer, for their careful reading of various chapters.

To Walter Brueggemann, the very words of whose many writings have become an intimate part of my own voice and whose ideas pervade much of this book. Thank you for your commitment to excavating the truth of the Bible.

To my editors at Resource Publications, Kathi Scarpace and Bill Burns, for their patience and diligence. To the editor of the *Franciscan* magazine for permission to reproduce material in Chapter Three from my article that originally appeared in Vol. 17, No 2, May 2005.

And finally, and most of all, to my incredible wife Jayne Prestwood and to my wonderful daughters: Laura, Fiona, and Hannah—heartfelt thanks for their love, friendship, and encouragement.

Terry Biddington
The Feast of the Birth of Mary
and the anniversary of my baptism, 2009

Introduction

The idea of risk-shaped discipleship is more than mere rhetoric. All discipleship needs to be risk-shaped if it is to truly respond to the challenge of communicating hope for today's world and so make a tear in the everyday fabric of the normal human perception of reality. This perception is everywhere colored by the deep hues of anxiety, fear, and pessimism.

The communication of hope creates a space in which to articulate a voice that performs a different tune, a voice that calls us to participate and cooperate with God's endless creativity in an attitude of almost playful risk or daring. Hope is like the music of great jazz musicians; any so-called wrong note or mistake is immediately incorporated into the performance and becomes the basis for a new improvisation. While such an approach tests the musicians' ingenuity to its limits and is not without its risks, it gives them scope and impetus for the further creative development of their performance.

Similarly for us in the performance of our lives, hope exists when God and people together create an improvised response to the events and personalities, the joys and tribulations, of daily life. To understand the performance of human life as the risk-shaped challenge of hopeful improvisation is to understand that life is best appreciated as the result of the creative interplay between the nonnegotiable chords (the "givens" of our lives) and those gratuitous moments of serendipity, coincidence, or pure grace. In these moments of grace, our perception is momentarily but irrevocably transformed by the "yet-more" of God. And Scripture shows us that the Christian life is all about improvising on this score of hope, personified in Jesus' performance of his own life.

There is encouraging evidence (scriptural and otherwise) that God chooses to operate precisely through times of unimagined change and radical novelty, and that life is best understood from the perspective of constant renewal, newness, and new birth. The challenge of Christian discipleship is to look for the unexpected and the new and to discover divinity within it. We Christians today, perhaps as never before, are being called to consider how our world (which we think we know so well) and the church (which so many of us struggle to remain part of) may be imagined differently through the eyes of God.

In many parts of the world, the church has led the way in communities where suffering, exploitation, alienation, and abuse are rife. But the church in the West now needs to respond afresh to God's call by helping the world to discern how and where God is at work. Specifically, the church needs to help the world to *imagine into being* a different future by helping the world to hear the transgressive tales and subversive memories of a radically alternative way of life that it has been given to share. For the church has treasures that the world needs right now for its flourishing. It is only when the church rediscovers the radical newness of God and manages to live and share this revolutionary inheritance that it can be most true to its prophetic vocation in the world.

This book explores how we might collectively imagine new ways of being church and new ways of being true to the radical proclamation of Jesus of Nazareth. Each chapter begins by reflecting on a scriptural witness and then explores how to reexamine the relationship between traditional theological themes and our lived experience. This examination is done in the light of a renewed understanding of God as one who exists by birthing new life into being.

Chapter One explores the nature of change. All too often the church's reaction to change has been to avoid it at all costs. But if the church is to be true to its calling, it should itself become an agent of the freedom and change the world needs to experience.

Chapter Two explores freedom from anxiety and death through the story of Abraham and Sarah. It presents the birth of Isaac and the covenant as touchstones for discovering a life-giving mutuality between God and humanity. This chapter also examines the incarnation and birth of Jesus in order to show how each moment of our lives can be an opportunity to engage with the radically re-creative energy of God.

In Chapter Three we look at the great narrative of Moses and Aaron. These men speak God's truth to the powerful of their day through the proclamation of a radical alternative reality embodied in the Law given at Sinai. This Law, which was utterly different from any other, can paradoxically function like any law in its ability to create an inclusive identity and exclude people. This chapter explores how the Law must be challenged in the name of God if it is to reveal the real freedom that comes with risking all to be a disciple and follower.

What precisely this risk might entail is investigated in Chapter Four through the story of Jeremiah. The word of God that comes to Jeremiah is meant for those at the center of the political and religious life of Judah, a life focused on the temple and its rituals. Complete allegiance to unchanging practices and routines was believed to guarantee God's protection, even in the face of the undeniable chaos of the time. It was to be the solution to all the nation's security fears and problems. At the heart of this story is the showdown between Hananiah, the prophet of the establishment, and Jeremiah, the dangerous outsider, who represent two versions of reality and two visions of God.

The possibility of discovering the "yet-more" of God is

developed in Chapter Five from the curious idea found in Isaiah of the "treasures of the darkness." While the notion of darkness has frequently suffered negative overtones within the Jewish and Christian religions, its use in Isaiah opens a doorway to think about the hiddenness and essential unknowability of God. This chapter explores the wordless and imageless experience of darkness as the location for fresh and intimate encounters with God in the very ground of our being.

The next two chapters consider Jesus as the expression of God's newness and re-creative love. Chapter Six develops the idea of healing and the relationship between human bodies and the physical presence of Jesus. How is it, for example, that wherever Jesus goes he embodies in his own person the re-creative energy of God and turns *no-bodies* into *some-bodies*; that he calls forth from individuals an unexpected realization of their own visceral connectedness that draws them to membership in a community; that this community witnesses to the new reality bursting into the world and overcomes the simple dichotomy between "savior" and "saved"?

How the church might practice a theology of "fullness of life for all" is the theme of Chapter Seven. This chapter explores the way Jesus read and interpreted Scripture, how the early church reacted, and whether or not we might regain the practice of reading Scripture subversively. Imagination is essential to the work of doing theology and to the business of cooperating with God to help usher in the new values and practices of God's reign. For too many of us, Scripture has assumed a state of fundamental and irredeemable fixedness within our liturgical and ethical practice, which contributes to the bored indifference and lack of anticipation with which we routinely approach such amazingly life-giving texts.

Consequently, the church must repent and experience afresh

the re-creative love of God in order to create new strategies for offering the transformative care the world needs. Chapter Eight is an attempt to articulate a practical spirituality of risk and change. This chapter asks why we find ourselves so settled on the idea that truth is always timeless and changeless, and why we have allowed ourselves to become suspicious of being open (or opened) to change and growth. It also explores what can help us to confront our risk aversion and so enable God to help us rediscover what the church is for, what Christianity is to become in the West, and whether or not authentic risk-shaped discipleship is the real Christian vocation today and God's new gift to the world.

Each chapter and section conclude with questions with which to reflect, alone or with others.

Taking Stock of Where We Are: The Reality of Change

We in the West are aware, more acutely than any of our forebears, of being caught in the effects of change. We experience firsthand how technological development drives change at a faster rate than ever before and how the world is a "global village," with anywhere connected to everywhere. We are deluged indiscriminately every day with information from cyberspace. The news, flashed continuously across the surface of the planet, allows the impact of even relatively small events to affect people instantaneously on the other side of the world. Many of us in the West know personally and intimately how change affects our lives as we daily and routinely encounter all manner of difference: new languages, ideas, technologies, commodities, ethnicities, and religions in a way that would have been impossible in an earlier time. And rapid global change is just as real for rural living as it is for urban life.

Is this world we experience a "better" world? Not just better in the sense of fewer material hardships for those who can avoid them, but is it better in terms of *greater justice* for all, *fairer access* to education, health, and economic resources? Are there more employment opportunities? Do people have safer, more peaceful and hospitable places in which to live? Are we a happier and more fulfilled people because of the changes we experience? Despite all the material advances and "improvements" to our lives, the answer appears to be negative.

Walter Brueggemann, the American biblical scholar and

preacher, has often characterized the twenty-first century Western world as a world enthralled with militarism and consumerism. He sees us Westerners as entirely dependent upon therapeutic and technological solutions to our moral and spiritual dilemmas. We no longer feel at home in the universe; we are ill at ease and alienated from nature and from a sense of our shared vocation as human beings. According to Brueggemann, our existential angst drives us to seek security by stockpiling arms, seeing enemies behind every bush, and making adversaries of anyone who differs from us. We compensate for this *dis*-ease through materialistic living, consumerism and "retail therapy," through quick-fix chemical and medical treatments for our psychosomatic ills, and through technologies that remove us further and further from our connectedness with the earth.

The rapid change of our lifestyles has, not unsurprisingly, also impacted church life. Sunday church attendance has plummeted in many communities. The average age of parishioners is so high that the majority of clergy might now be said to be chaplains to the elderly and the dying. As a result of declining membership, most clergy and church leaders have—reluctantly or not—become conscious of their role in facilitating change. And most churches are slowly facing the fact that they need to change or they will die.

Yet all too often churches and congregations respond to change by piecemeal approaches that habitually bring frustration at the grassroots level and a sense of wasted opportunity in the wider church. There is no vision. Strategies for change rarely seem to emerge from an engaged theology that understands the processes of change and that has a robust spirituality that values change and risk as doorways to the most potentially creative places of encounter with God.

"Downsizing," "pruning for growth," and "pastoral reorganization," as the closure or amalgamation of churches and parishes is euphemistically called, is generally felt as negative. Change is something we do "reluctantly" or "at the end of the day," or "because there is no viable alternative." For Christianity, which is so fundamentally oriented to the future, to hope, resurrection, and the afterlife, this seems a very curious attitude. The business of change could be so profitably promoted as an opportunity to encounter afresh the God "who gives life to the dead and calls into existence the things that do not exist" (Rom 4:17). Change could be readily interpreted as the process by which God calls us to be co-creators and justice-makers.

Yet churchgoing Christians are notoriously averse to change. There is actual statistical proof that the church attracts society's natural conservatives. These conservatives are the so-called "guardians" who like the "traditional and proper" way in which things are done. They make up more than 50 percent of the churchgoing population and give rise to the widespread supposition that the overwhelming majority of churchgoers are unable or reluctant to change. It is often the case that when a change is suggested, no one is ever surprised to hear someone say, "Why do we have to change?" or, "We tried that before, years ago, and it didn't work" or else, "You just try *explaining* that to the congregation!" (One church even had someone object to the introduction of toilet facilities on the grounds that they had always managed without one in the past, so why change now?)

The nature of change

Change, of course, is a complex matter and managing the process of change is difficult. Change requires not only clear understanding and careful planning, but also the agreement, cooperation, and commitment from the bulk of those involved in and affected by the change. Change takes various forms, typically—in the language of systems theory:

- *incremental* change that aims simply to improve certain aspects of an organization or situation;

- *transitional* change that seeks to reach a new but known and desired state; and,

- *transformational* change that identifies the necessity for a change (although people may not know the final shape or direction of the change until it emerges from the remains of the previous chaotic, moribund, or ineffective state).

Transformational change is *radical*—reaching from or to the roots. This kind of change requires a shift in the assumptions (the underlying values and outlook of the organization and its members) as well as recognition of the way in which these assumptions may have outgrown, limited, or undermined real effectiveness. Transformational change also requires an organization's willingness to find ways of staying true to its foundational texts (vision, purpose, mission statement) and to its corporate memory and traditions. This faithfulness to the core texts, mission, memory, and tradition is accomplished by reexamining each of them, which can lead to new, alternative, and creative readings and responses that bring fresh energy, new direction, and organic revitalization.

Secular systems theory and business practice identify various models for engaging with change. Although the church might be said to be a *corporate body* and not a business as such, there are some fascinating and transferable insights between the world of business and church. Johnson and Scholes' "cultural paradigm," for instance, pictures an organization as composed of six elements or dynamics:

- stories and myths,

- symbols,

- rituals and routines,

- organizational structures,

- power structures, and

- control systems. (Johnson and Scholes 238)

Each element or dynamic interlinks and interacts with the others to create the organizational culture. Change in one dynamic can affect not only the whole, but also any of the other dynamics, as well as the equilibrium between them all. Also helpful is Lewin's three-stage paradigm for modeling change: the need to "unfreeze" the existing equilibrium, to identify a new position, and finally to "refreeze" the organization at a new point of balance (Lewin passim).

Helping people change

Managing transition is a costly activity. It involves helping people understand what has gone wrong with the existing ethos, structures, and practices and then helping them face up to the necessity of change. As with any ending or letting go, a change inevitably results in feelings of loss, grief, and anger. There is a need, therefore, for a time of careful—and caring—readjustment that allows people to grow into and accept a new identity. This time of growth is necessary before any positive ideas about new beginnings can be fully felt, expressed, and implemented.

During periods of change people need to be encouraged to reflect—alone and together—on the meaning of the past and how things might be in the future. They need to learn to resist the natural desire to view the past through rose-tinted spectacles or to anticipate the future with undue pessimism. In a time of change, as ever, mutual or group support is vital; it not only gives people space to discuss and critique the nature and content of the new regime and what it means for them and for their sense of belonging, but support also provides a means to explore the points of continuity with valued tradition.

At a time of change it is important to identify those who find real difficulty in accepting change and those who actively resist it in order to find ways of increasing commitment and ownership of the need for change. People resist change for many reasons: feelings of loyalty to the past, adherence to traditional forms of belief and action, an unwillingness or inability to face the issues, conflicting interests, apathy or a lack of engagement, misguided understanding of the issues, values, and purposes of the organization—or the simple dogged determination not to conform. Some people are just plain "changeaphobics" who will do anything to stay as and where they are.

Articulating a new way of being is of the utmost importance. It is also important to help people see how change can spring from (and is faithful to) the past and to see that change is a necessary response to the needs of a new environment and context. Recognition that loyalty to the past can also mean the acceptance of a fresh approach is an essential understanding to reach because it releases fresh energy and enthusiasm.

While the above insights and analogies assume only human agency to be at work, they do nevertheless clearly highlight the absence of a thoroughgoing practical theology and spirituality of change within the church (or at least the absence of an articulation of a practical theology and spirituality of change at the grassroots level, where creative participation in the shaping of mature and imaginative theological responses to change matters infinitely more than many of our church leaders ever appear to imagine).

Church as an agent of change

In contemporary theology God's changelessness is rarely critically investigated. In times of change, it is always important to affirm that God will sustain us as we cross boundaries and to understand that God draws us into the uncertainty of the future. But given the immense changes that confront the church today, we can legitimately ask why there is so little in the way of a creative and accessible theology of change.

The church needs to offer resources to explore the importance of change using biblical narratives through the themes of creation, vocation, Exodus, and journeying. The church needs to challenge and encourage people to discover how openness to change can be regarded as virtuous discipleship just as much as constancy and faithfulness to the past are. And the church needs to articulate a spirituality that sees change as a natural part of human life, as a place of intimate encounter with God, and as a way to fulfill the vocation to creativity that we share with all people and that God shares with us. And we need to learn how to understand and value risk in order to imagine God's future into becoming. In short, congregations need help and training to handle the experience of change creatively.

If change is such an inevitable part of human life, then why are we so reluctant, hesitant, or downright opposed to it? Christian belief is filled with "new life," "new birth," and "new creation." Are we really all so naïve as to imagine that the church—even our own local church—will be exactly the same in a hundred, or even fifty years' time?

We must allow ourselves a little space in which to think about the future: about what might happen if we do nothing, and about what might happen if we open ourselves to imagining alternative hopes and expectations for God's church. After all, imagining things is surely halfway to enabling them to come to be.

Your experience of change

In a time of silence you may now wish to consider your answers to the following questions. If you are with others in a group you may choose to share your responses with them.

- What things have changed in your lifetime? Would you say the world is a better place to live or would you agree with Brueggemann that we are in confusion and denial?

- What has changed in your church during your time? Who or what drives the need to change in your church? How is change discussed in church meetings or from the pulpit?

- How might your church respond to the anxiety and injustice that exist in the world? How does your church try to engage with the big issues in your local community? What do you try to do yourself?

- What do you think that the Christian faith has to say about change? What stories or ideas can you find in Scripture or in church teaching that you might want to share with others about change?

Chapter 1-B

Imagining Things Differently: Newness and the Experience of God

Let us now explore some ideas about change, newness, and God—that is, the experience of God in or as "newness," as novel, different, utterly unexpected, and totally astonishing. Let us explore how God hovers restlessly at the creative interface, the cutting edge, the growing point, and the crossing place. What resources of imagination and courage are required as we set about—as we must—venturing everything we hold dear in order to rediscover God at moments and places of risk where the predictable present meets the possibility of disruptive newness?

What might these risks mean for us, for our churches and communities, and for our world?

Another kind of a guide

Many of us are all too aware, as we listen to sermons, take part in study groups, or worship and share life in the Christian community, that there is a great weight of tradition that seems to dominate our living and thinking about the Christian life. Our reference points are all from the past, from a different world. In the Anglican Church we talk of locating ourselves with respect to Scripture (the biblical texts), tradition (the body of past theological and biblical interpretation), and human reason (the need to use our God-given wits). We believe it is essential to do everything we can to engage intellectually and prayerfully with the witness of our Scripture and with the ways in which Christians have interpreted the texts over the two millennia. These three things: Scripture, tradition, and reason serve as essential springboards as we go about the business of reflecting on our theology and integrating it with our pastoral care.

But what value do we give to our actual *experience* of living in today's world? Why does personal, lived experience count for so little alongside Scripture, tradition, and reason? Why do we so reluctantly start from our embodied experience as the basis for developing our theological reasoning, our spiritual practice, and our ethical living in the context of the challenges of our life today?

The answer, of course, is that we generally refuse to believe that our experience might legitimately and meaningfully serve as the way God and the things of God are revealed. After all, we say, to trust our experience is surely to open the floodgates to the self-delusional and to the whims of the aggrieved and the downright evil among us. But this same trust also opens the floodgates to experience of the mystics, the social outcasts, those with disabilities, and all those so-called minorities in our society whose experience differs from our own.

We dread the challenges of interacting with newness, difference, and otherness. Why should this be so? We must realize that we cannot face the unknowable risks of the future simply by taking refuge in the certainties of the past and in the faith of those who have gone before us. But we *can* commit ourselves to active theological, spiritual, and intellectual engagement with our experience of life *and so open ourselves to the unpredictability of the future.* And as we grapple with the big issues of our faith that matter so much to us, this willing engagement so very often leads us to new discoveries, radical wonder, and transformative encounters with the divine.

Do we really mean to say that there is no space for God to enter, challenge, and transform our lives in the here and now? Is God's revelation all over and done with? Are the only tasks required of us today a sifting of the historic facts (from the Latin *factum* meaning "done" or "finished"), a continual routine rereading of God's completed dealings with humanity and a random dipping into the hodgepodge of others' past beliefs in our attempts to illuminate our own very different context? Is God's truth already revealed to us in its entirety or is God's revelation also ongoing and open-ended?

The idea of God as "the divine ever beyond our knowledge and imagination" (as St. Anselm said), suggests that there is room for us, alone and with those who hold perspectives that differ from our own, to explore (and perhaps lay aside) theories, hypotheses, and models. And as we engage with issues of contemporary faith and life, we must learn to be open to the "yet unimagined," to the "completely unexpected," to the "new" and "what-might-still-be"—the "yet-more" of God.

God, change, and church

We have such an ambivalent understanding of change. On the one hand, words such as eternal, everlasting, infinite, and perpetual are often used to describe the character of God. Such descriptions can mistakenly imply changelessness in the sense that God's actions never alter. On the other hand, the idea of change can suggest imperfection, inadequacy, unreliability, and untrustworthiness. But both approaches miss the point. Though God's commitment to the covenant with humanity is steadfast, *God's essence resides in change.* Just as God can no more cease to create and call new things into being, so God cannot cease to call us who are made in God's image, to change, to grow, and to journey beyond our present horizons.

We say that Jesus is a living reality and that the Spirit of God is the ever-present guide who leads us into new life; and yet we seem unwilling to trust in what we say we believe. We hesitate to explore the new ideas and practices that might come from having an embodied, dynamic faith. We prefer instead to keep Jesus and his inescapably radical message safely locked up in the pages of Scripture: just text, just words, just stories. And any preacher who has dared parishioners to step outside the boundaries of their accustomed understanding of common biblical texts, and challenged them *to actually hear something new*, something that might impinge their lives with new possibilities and fresh understandings of God, will know the likely reaction. Far too many churchgoers consider the biblical narratives, by virtue of their being in the Bible, to be of even less material relevance than other peoples' lives they may read about in magazines. People simply do not, on the whole, go to church expecting to engage with something quite new and utterly unexpected that will open up a different world before their eyes.

All too often people's experience of church seems to lead them to imagine that the Word never actually became human flesh or made a difference at all, but instead is merely an idea that they can choose to assent to intellectually (or not). Or else people believe that the proclamation of the resurrection of Jesus—mumbled in an embarrassed way for a few weeks after Easter—has neither real currency in the big world outside of church, nor any tangible, meaningful impact on the sort of people they are called to become.

This incapacity to recognize and to live the true value of what we have received and our aversion to change and openness to the "what-and-where-next-of-God," are precisely the things that stop so many people on the outside of church—those who are open, concerned, passionate, and curious about life, those who are needy and ill-treated in society, and those who have lapsed, given up, outgrown, or become impatient—from ever being tempted back.

For too many people—churchgoers included—there is nothing very much on offer in church. Nothing appears to make much of a difference to those who actually attend. There is no creative impact on the local community and no obvious point of connection with the real world and its problems. So people go off and are active outside the church, where the Holy Spirit is alive and well. How much we have to learn! How much we need to change!

The Body of Christ

We say we are the Body of Christ. If we want the Body of Christ to grow and thrive in our contemporary climate of exponential change and if we want our Christian communities to exist in the future, then we need to imagine, create, and develop new embodied spiritual practices and theological understandings. These new disciplines of thought and action will enable us to articulate our discoveries about God and God's revelation made through our experience. These discoveries will lead us to ask probing questions about the boundaries to the Body of Christ and—*if there are boundaries*—about their location, nature, and function. Is the Body of Christ one that is open to what is outside and around it? Is its skin porous enough to allow it to breathe and grow and receive nourishment from the world in which it exists? And where and how does this Body experience pain and need healing?

There is renewal and growth in the church, if we know where to look. The Spirit of God is always eager to lead the church further, despite the best indifference, reluctance, and resistance it can collectively muster. People encounter the Christian message in a wide variety of ways, across the theological spectrum from the popular "Alpha" to the "Emmaus" courses and in many planned and unplanned ways, but the past still dominates. The problem is that regular churchgoers and new attendees alike are too often offered uncritical "re-presentations" of established theological ideas: bundles of well-tested truth propositions, biblical quotations, and ethical positions focused on personal piety and individual discipleship. There is only occasionally real encouragement to think seriously about, or to be actively involved in, the big justice issues facing their world.

People need to be persuaded to go beyond superficiality and self-centered commitment: to find something that will encourage and empower them to think critically, creatively, and *theologically* for themselves, as they set off on the journey towards the God who is forever-coming-to-birth and demanding justice for the world.

What is the Christian journey like?

Some people prefer to carry a heavy rucksack of baggage from the past and to travel with others along familiar pathways with a simple map or to travel on a predetermined route. There is a

pressing need, however, for the church to engage, encourage, and
equip those who choose to travel entirely alone, well beyond
recognizable coordinates, deep into the darkness and the
unknown. For such adventurers what is needed is not a map but a
chart describing the likely features of the terrain, as well as the
encouragement to explore it themselves. And on this journey they
need, not an approved universal package of rations, the "milky
food" (1 Cor 3:2); they need something that can get their teeth
into. Real spiritual nourishment. They also need light, flexible
rucksacks to fill with the new things they discover as they go
forward into new encounters and experiences of God and to new
experiences with the divine revealed in and through the journey
into their humanity. Indeed, many people today are less concerned
with a safe arrival after death in some heavenly paradise than with
experiencing the fullness of eternal life here and now. For such
people, it is not the destination but the journey that counts.

Shouldn't the church make more of an effort to give people,
not only the critical tools to deepen their knowledge of God, but
the encouragement to develop the needful gifts of faith and
courage to appreciate the "yet-more" riskiness and strangeness of
God? Shouldn't the church encourage the use of creative
imagination to investigate those times and places where everything
we know and value seems set to disintegrate and unravel? For
these places are exactly where the ever-radically transformative
love that is God can be most fully recognized. The very processes
of change we see around us, the "cutting edge of things," are the
places where God's newness is most readily encountered.

Cooperating with God in the birthing of newness

Little attention is paid to the idea of the radical newness of
God. Very few Christians promote an understanding of God's ways
through the experience of new ideas and practices, through times

of change, and at those *very moments in time when future becomes present.* Academic theologians may talk of God's transcendence and immanence and of God being eternally present, "provisionally" and "contingently." Great spiritual writers may talk about encountering God in the "sacrament of the present moment." The notion that God is always more on the cutting edge of our lives than God is in our past, or that God exists by forever coming-to-birth in each new change and challenge, is seen, however, as a novel or possibly even an odd and dangerous concept. Our past theological understandings need to be under constant review and our faith needs to be forever "worked at," and engagement with change (whether it be new experiences, situations, dilemmas, or challenges) cannot be ignored for ignoring change means ignoring the place where God is most clearly found at work.

On one level, encountering God in the processes of change is a way for us to discover and faithfully live out our discipleship. On another level, the encounter with God in change represents a way in which the church can fulfill its prophetic call to serve as spiritual beacon both to its members and to the world beyond. On a third level, it is just possible that if we dare to reexamine and modify our dependence on the past and learn to discern God's presence at the very point we feel that deep waters are about to break over our heads and drown us all, we might find that, instead of drowning, we are riding atop a wave that will carry us forward and enable us to cooperate with God in bringing about God's yet unimagined newness.

The gift of imagination

As hard as it may be for us to envisage new things, we must try to do so, for it is clear that imagination is a profoundly life-giving asset when it comes to studying Scripture or doing theology. Imagination is not the dreadful taboo many traditionally fear it to be by virtue of its superficial association with fantasy. Imagination is an integral part of our God-given identity; it is the interface between us and God, the very touchstone for divine activity. Imagination is the means whereby God rearranges our "mental furniture" so as to enable us to see, think, and act as God does.

It may, of course, feel a very daunting task to consider how we might begin to *imagine God's future into being*.

For one thing, we may imagine, at some cost to ourselves, God's reality to be radically different than what we thought it to be. We may need to discover that when we are willing to imagine what seems humanly impossible, inconvenient, or even undesirable, our imagination actually creates a space within us that allows God's newness to be born. Every occasion for grappling with change and for opening ourselves to the risks and uncertain outcomes of change becomes an opportunity for us to work with God as co-creators of our communities and of our world. Likewise, every act of our God-given capacity to imagine a radically different future may become the very means of discerning the Spirit of God asking us to risk, grow, and change.

A framework for change

In her book *A Feminist Ethic of Risk*, Sharon Welch talks of the need for a matrix of strategic risk-taking, a framework that offers a way forward for social and political action. Welch proposes a framework for discerning change and risk and for testing and measuring them against a set of indicators or benchmarks, specifically how change and risk might work for justice, for the flourishing of individuals and communities, and the ecosystem itself (Welch 46). Her framework is one that seeks to value:

- the particular and partial, instead of the monolithic;

- that which is contingent and specific to one time and place, instead of the permanent and unquestionable;

- that which is fluid and flexible, dynamic, and transformative; and,

- the interdependence of different groups and individuals, which is welcoming of difference and diversity. (Welch 136)

Would it be possible to develop a similar framework to use as a tool for discerning spiritual risk–taking? Is there a way to encourage people to overcome their anxiety in order to welcome change and engage creatively with it? What would such a framework look like? This book will explore the implications of such a matrix.

Time to think about your own experience

In a time of silence you may now wish to consider your answers to the following questions. If you are with others in a group you may choose to share your responses with them.

- Do you think that your experience should have an equal place alongside Scripture, tradition, and reason in shaping theology? Why or why not? What concerns might people have about experience? Do you think that God is revealed in all human experience, or are there limitations?

- In your discipleship how do you balance the need for doctrine alongside the idea that Christian faith is a grand adventure in living and in discovering what it really means to be human?

- Where do you experience God today? In what parts of your life is it difficult to find God?

- Should the church reexamine the source and nature of its certainties and change some of its thinking in order to reconnect with people? Do you think the rest of the world is out of touch with Christian teaching?

Abraham and Sarah: From Anxiety to New Birth

As a sprightly seventy-five-year-old, Abram set out from his father's home to the land of Canaan. There is no question in the text that seventy-five was late to be starting a risky journey into the desert. Neither is there any hint that he was not really quite settled in Haran. He left in response to God's call.

Did he simply go because it was God who called or did he go because of a sense of adventure and discovery? Abram was no regular hero; like many people of faith, he was a complicated character with a deep anxiety about life in general. Perhaps the real reason he left, hinted at time and again, was actually because he was mortally anxious about his future. He was worried about the survival of his name and line. He left because God promised that, if he made it to Canaan, his fears would be no more.

> "I will make of you a great nation, and I will bless you, and make your name great, so that you will be a blessing."
> (Gen 12:2)

Like any of us, no doubt Abram's motives were mixed. Perhaps there were others whom God had called previously and who had ignored the summons or, like Abram's father, who had settled down for good. Abram could have chosen to stay at home, but he went nonetheless. He said "yes" to God. Abram has a story to tell us about overcoming anxiety, about undertaking something risky and new at any stage of life. He can tell us about an adventure that exceeded his wildest imaginings. An adventure *on the far side* of his fear.

Setting off to build a new life in a new place is always a hazardous business. This is no less the case for Abram, not only because God was rather vague about the location of this new land (Gen 12:1), but also because Abram was wealthy. Abram had many possessions and slaves and had a great deal to lose. Although he was devout and built sacrificial altars to God as he journeyed through Canaan to the Negev desert, what was the real extent of his religious practice? Was he like many of us who pray or carry medallions or crucifixes when we travel? How was he influenced by his deep-seated anxiety about his future security? Did he feel compelled to placate God with sacrifices in order to remind the Almighty about the promise of a new home for him and his people? For everywhere he journeyed, Abram discovered that the land seemed to be already quite crowded with other people. Perhaps there will be no room for him; perhaps he misheard God's travel directions. Perhaps.

Abram in Egypt

Abram appears to be an anxious man, and this existential angst and pathological fear are illustrated in a number of episodes in the Genesis narrative. The first example is the curious incident in which he tells his wife Sarai that she must pretend to be his sister (Gen 12:10–20). The story begins with the arrival of Abram and Sarai in Canaan, where there is a famine. Abram's trust in God evaporates. His fear, that Canaan is no place to start building the great dynasty God promised, causes him to press on south towards Egypt, the famous land of plenty. But each step he takes increases his sense of impending doom (and our own, as we recall the famine during Joseph's time that led the Hebrews into Egypt and eventual slavery).

At the frontier, Abram's fears again overwhelm him. The Egyptians might kill him (the Hebrew has "slaughter him" graphically indicating Abram's heightened fears for himself) and ruin all his hopes for the future. Before crossing the border, Abram tells Sarai: " 'Say you are my sister, so it may go well with me because of you, and that my life may be spared on your account' " (12:13). The Egyptians might kill him, he thinks, but with Sarai as his sister, they are bound to treat him reasonably. His fear readily drives him to use her as a bargaining chip, but the plan backfires, and Sarai is taken off to be Pharaoh's wife (12:19). God sends furious plagues upon the unwitting and deceived monarch until she is returned to Abram and they are deported forthwith back into the desert. How Abram's willingness to risk all he loves mirrors our own selfish foolhardiness!

Abram's dream

A second episode, years later, finds Abram still losing sleep because of his anxiety. Sarai had not conceived, and Abram's future hung in the balance. God reiterates the promise to bless Abram greatly in the land (Gen 13:14–18), but Abram is not happy. Quite the reverse: Abram is even more anxious: he did not have the heir he so desperately needed as he stood impatiently contemplating his own apparently fruitless future and approaching mortality.

One night Abram has an anxious dream, a vision in which he complains to God for leaving him without offspring and without any future in an alien land. In the vision God famously takes Abram outside the tent to look up at the night sky with its numberless stars and says:

"Look toward heaven and count the stars, if you are able to count them." Then [God] said to him, "So shall your

descendants be." And he believed the LORD; and the LORD
reckoned it to him as righteousness. (15:5–6)

Somehow Abram found it within himself to say "yes" to God,
just as he had done once before, long ago, in Haran. His rational
and angst-ridden self stilled in the dream; he took God at God's
word: there will be children. At last Abram understood that with
this God, who made the stars out of nothing, nothing is impossible.
God makes a promise, a covenant, with Abram as a permanent
mark of faithfulness to him and to his future descendants (15:18),
even though Abram can neither imagine the process nor the
outcome. How God will bring everything to pass was beyond
Abram's imagination. He only knew that he must take God's word
on trust, despite the fear and anxiety that continually ate away at
his insides.

Sarai's solution

However, it is Sarai who, knowing nothing of this covenant,
intervenes and preempts the fulfillment of the promise by persuading
Abram to take Hagar, her Egyptian slave woman as the mother of his
children (Gen 16:1–4). Facing her own anxiety, hurt, and pain at
being unable to have children, Sarai resolves her concerns for her
own future by offering Abram what she saw to be the only way
forward: surrogacy. Abram didn't argue; in the cold light of day,
wouldn't this surely be the obvious solution for him, too?

In stark contrast to Sarai's long years of fruitless trying, Hagar
immediately conceives. Hagar, who perhaps saw Abram as "her
man," began to disdain Sarai. Sarai's pain and resentment
overflows until she cracks. Hagar then runs away into the desert,
only to be found by an angel who tells her to return home and
submit (16:7–9), but not before making a promise to her:

"I will so greatly multiply your offspring that they cannot
be counted for multitude. … Now you have conceived and
shall bear a son; you shall call him Ishmael." (16:10–11)

God would use Hagar and her son in great ways, for it is from
them that all Arab peoples trace the line of their ancestry (but that
is another story). God has specific plans for anxious Abram,
although it would not be as either Sarai or Abram imagined.

Abram and a new covenant

A third episode begins in Genesis 17, some thirteen childless
years later. God reiterates the great nighttime covenant and promises
to make Abram's offspring "exceedingly numerous" (17:2). God then
transforms the verbal covenant into a covenant of flesh and blood.
God addresses Abram's anxiety directly by taking the words of the
promise (is it too absurd to imagine a certain irony here?) and
marking them in Abram's body where he can never forget them.
With each act of urination and intercourse, God has given Abram a
constant and tangible reminder to abandon fear about his future and
the fulfillment of God's promise of blessing. Abram has to agree that
all his male descendants will also be circumcised so that God's
faithfulness and promise of future security might never be forgotten.
And this sign of circumcision will serve as a permanent reminder for
his offspring for all generations.

God marks this new covenant on Abram's body and gives
Abram and Sarai new names and fresh identities. And, as though
this were not already enough, God promises Abraham that Sarah
will herself bear *from her own flesh* the son for whom they both
long. Abraham's anxiety erupts as bemusement, and he falls on his
face before God, laughing at the outrageous prospect of a
centenarian becoming a father.

Camping at Mamre

A fourth episode that illustrates Abraham's fear is the tale of the events at his camp by the oaks of Mamre in Hebron (Gen 18:1–15). Here God resolves, for good, the anxiety that both Abraham and Sarah felt about their future security, about children. At Mamre they come to understand exactly what God's blessing means and that their trust in God will be vindicated.

Abraham sits at the door of his tent in the heat of the day, and he sees three strangers. Immediately he offers water for their feet and food. After they finish, the strangers ask after Sarah, who is sitting behind the tent flaps. She hears one stranger tell Abraham that when he returns, she will give birth to a son. This announcement leads to the famous moment when Sarah laughs aloud, as Abraham had done. She laughs in the face of what she knew to be clearly impossible: "It had ceased to be with Sarah after the manner of women. So Sarah laughed to herself, saying, 'After I have grown old, and my husband is old, *shall I have pleasure?*'" (18:11–12, emphasis mine).

These foolish men! She has passed menopause and Abraham (as the New Testament writer of Hebrews suggests) is himself "as good as dead" (Heb 11:12). Her laughter prompts one of the strangers to address her: "'Why did Sarah laugh?' ... 'I did not laugh' ... 'Oh yes, you did laugh'" (Gen 18:13–15).

In the midst of this dialogue is the marvelous line God addresses to her: "'Is anything too wonderful for the LORD?'" (18:14). Is anything too difficult or impossible for God? As Sarah is soon to learn, there is really nothing impossible for the God who exists to create new life. The following year Sarah gives birth to Isaac and rejoices:

"God has brought laughter for me; everyone who hears will laugh with me." And she said, "Who ever would have said

to Abraham that Sarah would nurse children? Yet I have
borne him a son in his old age." (21:6–7)

God created what Abraham and Sarah thought to be beyond
the bounds of possibility: the marvelous flourishing of hope born
out of anxiety. This is the God for whom all things are possible and
who created something unimaginable for the mother and father of
God's people.

Isaac's birth is clearly a threshold moment in the Abraham
narrative. Abraham and Sarah, although open to setting off into
the desert at God's call and wandering anxiously toward an
uncertain future, nevertheless were hopelessly taken aback when
God's future collided with their reality in a twist entirely beyond
their wildest imagination. God did something utterly contrary to all
possible human expectations. There was not only the birth of a
new son and a promised future but an opening up from God's side
of a new way of relating to God, of a new way of understanding
God, of a new way for God to be God in the world. What
happened next is astounding.

Abraham's new freedom with God

After the three mysterious strangers were refreshed, they set
off with Abraham to Sodom where God (now revealed as one of
the three strangers) wants to see what exactly goes on there before
determining whether or not to punish the people for their
sinfulness. Now that Abraham is to be the father of a great nation,
God wonders whether to allow him to witness the operation of
God's justice (Gen 18:17–19). While the two others go ahead to
observe the city, God stays behind with Abraham who, in a
remarkable text, persuades God not to destroy it:

"Suppose there are fifty righteous within the city; will you
then sweep away the place and not forgive it for the fifty

righteous who are in it? Far be it from you to do such a
thing, to slay the righteous with the wicked, so that the
righteous fare as the wicked! Far be that from you! Shall
not the Judge of all the earth do what is just?" (18:24–25)

God agrees to do as Abraham requested, so Abraham presses
the argument further: Suppose there were forty-five? Forty? Thirty?
Twenty? " 'Oh do not let the Lord be angry if I speak just once
more. Suppose ten are found there' " (18:32).

Abraham bartered with God. Emboldened by the experience of
God's covenant and promise to him, Abraham had, it seems, finally
been able to overcome his deep-rooted anxiety. And out of this
newfound courage he did something entirely new. He persuaded
God to reconsider how a just God acts, to remember the demands of
God's justice, and to agree to be merciful. He managed to change
God's mind. He dared to risk the new covenant God made with
him—by holding God to it. Abraham tested the covenant to see just
what it was worth. He pushed at the boundaries of his new
relationship and found himself in a totally new territory.

Perhaps Abraham returned that day to his tent strangely
surprised at his own unexpected courage—where had that come
from? Perhaps he was also conscious that something utterly new
had happened. There was the astonishing announcement to Sarah
of an impending birth and the gift of victory over his own anxiety,
but also the feeling that he and God had stumbled into a new
dimension, that their relationship had been tested and had
evolved. God and humanity were in a new place together, a place
that was the real destination of his travels and of God's call.

This place was not a place of equality (for who is equal to the
living God?) but rather a place of newly-discovered mutuality, a
space in which God and Abraham might jointly create and articulate
a new relationship. Abraham, for his part, learned to respond to the

new things that God was now enabled to do and disclose by virtue of the novel and creative mutuality that their covenant birthed. If Abraham had not finally trusted the covenant, if he had not used his newfound freedom from anxiety as a springboard to empowerment (witnessed in his bargaining with God outside Sodom), who knows what might have happened? Would God have chosen that time, place, and relationship to disclose more about God's own being and the unfolding of God's purpose?

Test of a new relationship

Sooner or later, however, the mutuality of this new relationship between God and Abraham would inevitably mean that God would come to test Abraham. This drama is the fifth episode that relates Abraham's fear: the story of the sacrifice of Isaac (Gen 22:1–19), a text that is often denigrated as an act of callous abuse by God.

Early in Genesis 22, God calls Abraham to leave his camp and to offer his son as a sacrifice:

> "Take your son, your only son Isaac, whom you love, and go to the land of Moriah, and offer him there as a burnt offering on one of the mountains that I shall show you." (22:2)

By modern standards this request appears to be outrageous, but Abraham didn't flinch from carrying out the instructions. And just as God set off from Abraham's camp at Mamre to test the people of Sodom accompanied by two men, so now Abraham takes two men with him as he left for a testing of his own.

Climbing to the summit, Isaac asks what is to be sacrificed. Abraham's answer is ambiguous: " 'God … will provide the lamb for a burnt offering, my son' " (22:8). In terms of narrative, this is the most dramatic moment in the whole story of Abraham. How will he respond? Had he so completely overcome his former anxieties and reached such a place of calm and trust before God that he was now absolutely obedient in all things—even to the point of killing his son? Did he believe that the covenant would hold, that the God he had come to know was a God of justice and would indeed provide a lamb for the offering? Or was he avoiding his son's question and putting off the agony until the last moment? Had his former anxiety reasserted itself to get the better of him one last time?

Who could possibly predict the outcome as the knife trembled momentarily in Abraham's hand above his son's throat? The text itself suggests that Abraham seems prepared to go all the way. He "reached out his hand and took the knife to kill his son" (22:10). At this *cutting edge moment* in their relationship, both God and Abraham waited upon each other. Both seem prepared to risk what they have come to value. Abraham, as he held the knife point ready, contemplated the loss (by his own hand) of all that he and Sarah had most desired: offspring, security, future fulfillment, and blessing. On God's side, there was the real possibility that, if Abraham struck Isaac, this particular covenant and its promise would be extinguished; the new relationship God and Abraham had discovered would be lost forever.

Abraham tenses the muscles in his arm; instantly, an angel stays his hand. God, at last, speaks again to Abraham: "'... Now I know that you fear God, since you have not withheld your son, your only son, from me'" (22:12). Abraham passed God's test.

And it is equally possible to imagine that God passed the same test. For their relationship, though intact, is now different. Albeit God could have created other alternative outcomes, both had risked everything. By preferring the self-limitation of this particular time and particular relationship, God opted to ride the risk, as Abraham had done, and witnessed the birth of a new stage in their relationship. Perhaps it is this very moment at which God said "yes" to the recognition that the covenant would last—not because God willed it, but because Abraham committed himself freely to it.

Abraham discovered the "yet-more" of God just as his world was about to disintegrate around him. And God saw that the experiment of this time, this place, and this relationship had worked. So God repeats the blessing over Abraham and his descendants, a blessing that God now willingly extends to all the peoples of the world:

> "By your offspring shall all the nations of the earth gain blessing for themselves, because you have obeyed my voice." (22:18)

The man whose life was once in bondage to anxiety and timidity became, not exactly the perfect hero, but the means of blessing for countless generations to come. And God, the source of all blessing, discovered what surely God already suspected, that human potential for creative mutuality reveals that humans are made in God's own image.

Their story and our story

The story of Abraham and Sarah is the story of a journey; a journey that begins when they hear God's call to leave where they are, a call to let go of the things that hold them back—including the things they consider impossible to do and be—a call to become different people with new identities.

Their story is a powerful one for us today because it is a story about risk and daring, about working through human, mixed motives and overcoming fear, about learning to trust that God is with us on the journey. It is a story about realizing that the destination, the endpoint, might be uncertain or seem unattainable, that God's call might demand that we have the courage to think the unthinkable and to enter strange new places and situations of unimaginable risk.

Abraham and Sarah's story dares to articulate something not often realized about the character of God: God, who holds the destiny of all things in a hand, is willing to work with the unpredictability of human action in such a way so as to *improvise creatively*. God brings something entirely new and wholly unexpected to birth out of the "dangerous edge of things" (to quote Robert Browning), out of each uncertain moment and each dubious outcome.

Their story illustrates the demands of the journey of faith we each must make in our own time. With God's help, we will encounter and overcome our fears and anxieties as we travel through time as the often indecisive, anxious, and frequently confused church community.

Time to think about your own experience

In a time of silence you may now wish to consider your answers to the following questions. If you are with others in a group you may choose to share your responses with them.

- Have you reflected recently whether or not the place you are is still where you are meant to be? How might you begin to do this?

- What is your experience of encountering unfamiliar people, new ideas, and unexpected possibilities? Do you recognize the anxiety Abraham and Sarah felt? How might you use their story to help you with yours?

- How do you deal with change? Do you avoid it at all costs or rise to the challenge? What changes might be on the agenda for your church or community? How can you begin to think aloud about change by yourself or with others? How can you discern new possibilities for life?

- Are there issues that you want to challenge God about? How might you go about holding God to the covenant of blessing and justice that Abraham and his offspring were promised?

A Time for New Birth:
Natality *as a Way of Re-imaging*
the Christian Adventure

How can our faith and trust in God speak to those issues that prevent us from living eternal life in the here-and-now? How can we avoid seeking safety through an overreliance on material things, through an overwhelming desire for intellectual certainty, or through a need for a tangible sense of cast-iron security? Why do we Christians, of all people, find it so very difficult to travel hopefully on the "dangerous edge of things"?

Learning from Abraham and Sarah

The story of Abraham and Sarah touches our story in several ways. The story is about two people who grow from anxiety into trust. Their anxiety about life in general and the future in particular may resonate with us because anxiety is a common and

crippling human condition. Anxiety challenges us, at a
fundamental level, to consider what it really means to live as
people of faith in a world of rapid change.

The story of Abraham and Sarah is also one that traces the
beginnings of critical self-awareness. They, like us, learned to
articulate who they were in relation to the God who "gives life to
the dead and calls into existence the things that do not exist"
(Rom 4:17). They struggled to realize that human flourishing lies
in trusting the present and future to the God who exists by
creating, and who needs to create and constantly bring new life to
birth *in order to exist at all.*

Their story demonstrates that God can be experienced afresh
at each new moment; that God comes to meet people each time
there is a risk to be encountered or a change to be negotiated,
each time the stability or security of life threatens to unravel. From
Abraham and Sarah we learn that God can be found at the very
point where everything feels as though it might disintegrate, at the
precise instant that the future appears about to collapse. We learn
that the presence of God is enough to ensure that any moment can
open out to embrace eternity.

Through their story we discover that the relationship between
ourselves and God is not one that is fixed or closed, but rather
porous, open to change and novelty. We learn that this
relationship is evidently mutual. It is a *heuristic* relationship, one
that is discovered and shaped, bit by bit, the more we travel in
each other's company, journeying together into the unknown. God
and Abraham tested and tried each other. God challenged
Abraham to leave the security of his home, to welcome the
outsider and stranger, to imagine an impossible future, and then to
risk losing the son who would guarantee that future. Abraham
challenges God to be the God who must—in ever new contexts—
create ways of living up to the demands of the covenant. Abraham

asks God to be a God who is forever oriented to the what-might-need-to-be-birthed. And God is willing to improvise each time things go awry.

God the improviser

Although the Bible is full of birth stories, Genesis—the "book of beginnings"—alternates between telling the stories of particular births and recounting the long lists of "begettings" that initiate and differentiate the various families within the nations. As the Hebrew Scripture unfolds, the story of God's people often develops when the smooth and expected progression of descent goes askew. God's plan goes forward despite whatever unexpected events threaten the future when an apparently secure future is overturned. To put it differently, the dance of time progresses even when the tune goes flat and God is forced to improvise some new melody in order to keep things moving.

For example, in Genesis 27 we learn that Jacob was given priority over Esau the firstborn, in Genesis 37 that young Joseph was selected over his older and more experienced brothers, and in Genesis 38:27 that there was a dramatic reversal in the birth order of Perez and Zerah. Likewise too, in the New Testament, the long genealogy of Matthew's Gospel (1:1–17) makes it clear that Jesus' extraordinary birth was prefigured in his own irregular and extraordinary genealogy. His ancestors include Tamar (seduced by her father-in-law), Rahab a prostitute, Ruth a foreigner, and Solomon, the son of Bathsheba, taken adulterously by David—all liaisons that were beyond the bounds of strict acceptability under the Law, all outside the anticipated conventions of a family pedigree.

All these unexpected occurrences, these radical discontinuities, prove to be *the very means* by which God gives new impetus to the story of God's dealings with the world. God responds to our continuous blunders and miscalculations, to those ruptures in the expected order, and works with the unanticipated: like a jazz musician improvising on whatever has gone before. God radically re-imagines the future by inviting us repeatedly to risk, to trust that God can work for and through us and our deliberate and accidental mistakes. For God's creativity is ever at work at the place of fracture and disintegration: the cutting edge, the point of growth, the "dangerous edge of things."

God the creator

The Bible is the story of ongoing creation: not of the "one-off" creation that superficial reading of Genesis 1–2 might suggest. The Bible reveals that God proceeds from creative act to creative act, from new birth to new birth: each bringing hope of life, fulfillment, and security, each offering us the means to be part of God's creative purposes in the world, the chance to be co-creators with God.

This creative impulse is both open-ended and oriented towards the future, yet it is also always and necessarily contemporary, always happening *now*, all around us. The creative impulse is the hallmark of a God who is the God of new life and new beginnings, who wishes for us to let go of our anxiety about life and to draw us instead into that creative way of seeing and engaging with the world. The future is a place, which, as each new scenario opens up, offers new possibilities for God and for us, new opportunities for examining our familiar narratives and expectations about who God is. The future is a place of new junctures and interfaces where God may disclose more new spaces for God's becoming. God who, against all our assumptions and expectations, has nothing to do with death. God who, in the act of consenting to the resurrection of Jesus, explodes death itself and births new life for the world.

Our fascination with mortality

The birth-oriented stories of the Bible stand in stark contrast to the long history of much Western philosophy. From Plato onwards it is clear that the inescapability of our mortality has been the dominant theme of Western thinking. Death and dying have preoccupied the greatest minds and have conditioned the way we see the world and shape our culture. Western civilization has been endlessly fascinated by a life-consuming dread of death. The West has developed theories of an afterlife and continually reinforced notions of eternity and eternal life. And Christianity in particular has even sought to *legislate* salvation by controlling access to the hereafter: heavenly bliss for the favored few and consignment to a hell of everlasting smoke, pain, and brimstone for the rest of us.

In the Western mindset, human mortality has created a profound sense of anxiety and thereby a consequent need for moral and intellectual certainty as well as a deep desire for security. And this anxiety has had wide implications. Fear of death has profoundly affected the way in which Western societies have conducted national policy and foreign relations. Western values promote exploitative and conflict-based economies at the expense of global justice and the environment and invest in military responses to difference and dispute to such an extent that it is impossible to consider any cultural history of the West without encountering deep-rooted notions of "outsider" and "enemy." It is impossible not to question the endemic impulse to domination, competition, mastery, conquest, and the use of lethal technologies to promote the Western agenda of national identity, security, and global "peace."

In essence, these responses to difference and dispute are acts of defiance against the real and ultimate enemy: death. We Westerners attempt to keep death as far away as possible, to keep it hidden, well outside the tranquil security of our myopic gaze. We surround death anxiously with taboos, routinely avoid discussing it, commit our physicians to prevail over it, and delay its arrival for as long as is (economically) feasible. If we have wealth, we may even dream of escaping it altogether by investing massive sums in cryogenic technologies or in space exploration in the hope of finding other worlds where, we imagine, death will somehow be denied. We defy death rather than take the opportunities we have for building life-affirming attitudes and practices and flourishing lifestyles and communities in the here and now.

Yet despite our best endeavors it remains apparent that, in the famous words of the philosopher Feuerbach, it is "death [that] gives meaning to life." Despite all efforts to the contrary, death is what really preoccupies our subconscious and our imaginations and ultimately distracts us from believing in life *before* death and the real demands of justice in and for the world.

It is imperative that we dare ourselves to step away from our increasingly neurotic preoccupation with physical mortality and free ourselves from the crippling anxiety that besets us. We must step away from death's intimidating mastery of our lives and try to look at things from a different angle. Can we see the world, not from the perspective of our inevitable death but from the perspective of our having been—really rather amazingly—born into the world? Can we not privilege our birth rather than the fact of our death and let go of the weight of our mortality altogether so as to surrender the debilitating affect that our mortality has on us? Can we cease to preoccupy ourselves with mortality and instead learn to focus our hopes on its opposite—*natality*—and so celebrate the preeminence of birth over death, of living over dying, of the embracing of fullness of life now over the hope of eternal life after death? It is a tall order; what exactly might it mean for us? And is it possible to shift our thinking in this way?

Choosing life

We have to search quite hard through the history of Western philosophy to discover people who have things to say about honoring life more than death. A good place to start is with the work of Hannah Arendt who was, until recently, better known as a pupil of the philosopher Martin Heidegger. Heidegger was a major exponent of the twentieth-century existentialist school of thought. Like Plato, Feuerbach, and others Heidegger held that, of all the things we can say about life, what is supremely incontrovertible is that human life is contingent, characterized by its finiteness and certain mortality. Heidegger's famous notion is that existence can be characterized as "being towards death," that our lives are totally conditioned by the inevitability of death. We are mortal. Born to die. Everything we know, feel or imagine follows from—and is in response to—this incontrovertible reality.

Arendt railed intensely against the idea that death encapsulates the whole reality of human existence. In *The Human Condition* she begins by acknowledging that the parameters of human life are indeed the facts of life and death, natality and mortality, and that, to a large extent, it is understandable that mortality has preoccupied human imagination. We cannot deny that we will all die:

> If left to themselves, human affairs can only follow the law of mortality, which is the most certain and the *only reliable law* of a life spent between birth and death. (Arendt 246, emphasis mine)

She suggests, however, that we need to ask whether humans attach such significance to this law for any other reason than because *men*, rather than women, have controlled the direction of philosophy and lawmaking. Men have shaped the content of human culture and society, and have deliberately downplayed the place of women and their role in childbearing, as well as ignoring the immense significance of the fact that human existence begins with physical birth.

Therefore, Arendt asks, what is the true significance of the immeasurable wonder of human birth? What are the implications of understanding that the real value and meaning of life arises from the fact of being born? Is it not perfectly possible to see life as the continuous flow of new birth and as the endless progression of myriad acts of coming to birth? Why should the end of human life be of any greater importance than its beginning?

Arendt concludes that it is rather birth, and not death, that has greatest significance in characterizing the human condition because "With the creation of man, the *principle of beginning* came into the world" (177). The fact that women are able to give birth to new life gives to humanity a facility for ever creating and embodying fresh beginnings: "the constant influx of newcomers who are born into the world as strangers" (9), whereby humanity is forever opening itself to newness, novelty, and difference. Arendt is convinced that this constant fact of new beginnings and new birth is:

> The miracle that saves the world, the realm of human
> affairs, from its normal, "natural" ruin ... the birth of new
> men and the new beginning, the action they are capable of
> by virtue of being born. Only the full experience of this
> capacity can bestow upon human affairs faith and hope.
> (247)

It is new birth, she argues, that brings a constant stream of new life and new beginnings into the world. It is new birth that endows humanity with a facility to engage with the continuous beginning of new things, new initiatives, and unexpected action. It is new birth that is the hope of humanity and that contains the real meaning of human life. The reality of constant new births, the birthing of children who will be different from their parents, with a different mix of genes and different life trajectories for the future, lends to humanity the characteristic ability to be open to all that is novel and new, unexpected and unknown—a characteristic that is not simply human but one that is derived from the very nature of the person and reality we call God. For God is forever open to responding to novelty in creation. And it is our openness to God's ceaseless novelty, to God's gratuitously wonderful acts, and to God's call for us to share in this venturesome creative risk-taking that has become dulled and buried under a shroud of anxious preoccupation. We are unable to reach out and trust that, in the words of Julian of Norwich, with God "All shall be well."

Arendt develops a life-affirming political philosophy based on this capacity for beginning anew. She considers labor, work, and action as the three most basic of human undertakings and that "The task and potential greatness of mortals lie in their ability to produce things—works and deeds and words" (19). She distinguishes however, between the ordinary capacity to labor for survival, to work, to make tools and objects, and even to shape culture and the ability to create *radical newness*, to create something that is unexpected, unforeseen, and "out of the blue," in her words "something new ... which cannot be expected from whatever may have happened before" (177). She talks of action rooted in new beginning-making as "the one miracle-working faculty of man" (246).

Jesus the beginner

The ability to make radically fresh beginnings through the enactment of love, forgiveness, and promise is, according to Arendt, Jesus' supreme discovery. In the course of a human ministry characterized by "wholeness-making," she sees Jesus as the embodiment of love (which "by reason of its passion, destroys the in-between which relates us to and separates us from others" [242]) and forgiveness ("the only reaction which does not merely re-act but acts anew and unexpectedly, unconditioned by the act which provoked it and therefore freeing from its consequences" [241]). Arendt also thinks that Jesus' capacity to make and fulfill promises or covenants is critical to his modeling and encapsulating the sole means that remedies the "unpredictability [and] the chaotic uncertainty of the future" (237). Because of his unconditional love, liberating forgiveness, and total trustworthiness, Arendt believes Jesus reveals what it means to re-imagine human life freed from anxiety and the fear of death. The task for us is to learn from Jesus how to be unbound from death and how to unbind God and call God forth from the tomb into which we continually place God.

For Arendt, Jesus' birth most fully captures the power of natality, of the ever fresh-birthed new beginnings that addresses our paralyzing preoccupation with death. For Jesus' birth brings:

> ... faith in and hope for the world that [finds] perhaps its most glorious and most succinct expression in the few words with which the Gospels announced their "glad tidings": "A child has been born unto us." (247)

If Arendt is correct that Jesus' *birth* offers humanity real hope for fullness of life, then why is it that the saving activity of God in Christ has been predominantly associated with Jesus' *dying* "once for all" on the cross rather than through his birth and incarnation in human form? Is it possible to ask whether, how, and to what extent, natality, birth, incarnation, and life in a physical body might be a valid and sufficient paradigm for revitalizing the Christian story of redemptive living for today's world? More fundamentally, can we ask why incarnation was even necessary, if God could forgive humanity at any point and in any way? What difference does incarnation actually make to the way we live our lives?

Jesus' birth as salvific

Hymns are always good indicators of the contemporary understanding of Christian faith, and Christmas carols are no exception. Of the many carols extant in the old hymnbooks, the modern practice is to sing only a handful of the most popular. These hymns are inevitably the ones that tend to focus on the Christ-child (for everyone likes a baby, we hear, and without children to receive presents "there would be no point in Christmas, would there?"). The hymns evoke a wistful desire for snow that is "deep and crisp and even," and a longing for a couple of restful "silent nights" after the stresses of the festive season. Christmas carols also mention that it was God's will that Christ was "born to die," although this idea is generally overlooked by the majority of churchgoers and preachers.

The thought that Jesus' physical birth and his human living is the means through which he offers us redemption or wholeness *by loosening the knots of the crippling angst that binds us* is nowhere to be found—despite originally being part of our theological tradition. For instance, the late second century theologian Irenaeus, Bishop of Lyons, saw Jesus' birth and incarnation as itself atoning by giving us a means of human encounter and friendship with God:

> The Lord has restored us into friendship through His incarnation … propitiating indeed for us the Father against whom we had sinned, and cancelling our disobedience by His own obedience; conferring also upon us the gift of communion with, and subjection to, our Maker. (Irenaeus 17.1)

Irenaeus believed that Jesus' exemplary life of obedience not only "satisfied" God by making up for Adam's disobedience, but also began a process of transforming humanity into divinity, converting mortal angst into the divine fullness or completeness. Christ became what we are in order that we might become what he is. The goal of the Christian life—as exemplified in Jesus' life and ministry—thus becomes the quest for the grace to become fully alive. Indeed, Irenaeus famously wrote that the glory of God is someone who is fully alive.

This idea of fullness of life was further developed by the fourth century theologian Athanasius, who understood Jesus' birth and incarnation as manifesting in flesh and blood the God who had hitherto remained hidden. He taught that Jesus' birth offers us a visible example of what "fully aliveness" might mean: the Word was made man in order that we might be made divine (Athanasius 54).

This goal of being fully alive suggests that the incarnation is a continuation of the ongoing process of creation, a process that will culminate in our divinization. Eventually we will be incorporated or enfolded into the full life of God, where death does not exist. In this model, creation begins with God who is fully alive, *speaking* and *creating* (the same verb in Hebrew) the world into being. Then, as Elaine Scarry observed, creation develops or unfolds through a gradual exchange between God and humanity. God, manifest in Genesis 1–2 as a disembodied voice relating to the world by speech and action upon the bodies of created forms, moves towards us while at the same time humanity, embodied but "voiceless" (in the sense of being unable to be creative like God) grows or is drawn toward God. The critical moment in this process is the birth of Jesus, when the disembodied voice of God takes on human flesh as the embodied Word. Through his life and ministry, Jesus enables voiceless humanity to speak and begin to realize its "fully aliveness" by acting upon the world as co-creators with God (Scarry 191-221).

Incarnation is thus a process in which God, through the action of embodiment in Jesus, discovers what embodied "creatureliness" feels like and signifies. And, in turn, incarnation enables humanity to enter into a renewed—"at-oned"—relationship with God. This relationship is no longer based on a sacrificial blood covenant or on the Law, with its view of human life in terms of categories of sinfulness, obedience, and disobedience, but on a relationship characterized by mutuality and friendship between God and humanity. We are co-creators, cooperating together and *risking the process* of giving birth to all that creates healing and enables life to flourish.

This may all seem a very long way from Abraham and Sarah. But their journey from anxiety to new birth, through their call to step with God into an unknown future, through learning to trust and risk what was utterly outside their imagination, is also our call to cooperative, venturesome love. We need to share this love with each other as we face the challenges of fitting the church for its vocation in the world and enabling it to articulate prayerfully, powerfully, and effectively a way out of anxiety and hopelessness. Speaking the truth that we have come to know in Jesus and daring to proclaim this truth in a world that has come to associate the church with outdated irrelevance is not a task for the fainthearted. But there is no possibility of hiding or shirking. All of us are called to this task, and all of us are sent out to speak and in so speaking, to help bring God's new reality to birth.

Time to think about your own experience

In a time of silence you may now wish to consider your answers to the following questions. If you are with others in a group you may choose to share your responses with them.

■   In what way might the concept of natality impact your
    view of death? What difference might it make to avoid
    using your energy and resources worrying and instead grant
    to death only the final act of your dying?

■   Have you ever had an encounter with God that radically
    changed a situation totally beyond your expectations?
    What happened? In what ways might your understanding
    of God in effect bind God so tightly that God needs to
    break free?

■   Have you ever wondered about your own creativity
    (however it manifests)? Have you thought of your
    creativity, not only as a gift from God, but as a way you
    share in God's creativity that opens up new possibilities for
    the future? How might this understanding of creativity
    change what "fullness of life" means to you?

■   Do you sometimes wish you had more faith? What exactly
    does that mean? Remember Jesus' words to Bartimaeus:
    "Your faith has made you *well*" (or "whole" or "saved you";
    see Mk 10:52). Why is it possible for remarkable things to
    happen when people share their faith with each other?

Moses—Exile, Identity, and Law: On Learning from a Burning Bush

Moses must have thought that his past was far behind him when he sat down to eat at Jethro's table and took a shine to Zipporah, one of Jethro's daughters. Very soon afterward Moses celebrated his deliverance and his good fortune by calling his firstborn "Gershom," meaning "I have been an alien residing in a foreign land" (Ex 2:21–22). Moses had indeed been an alien, but now as a member of his new family Moses could shepherd his father-in-law's sheep to his heart's content, safe from the trauma he experienced in Egypt.

Moses' story is very familiar. Born a Hebrew, he is raised as an Egyptian in Pharaoh's court, alienated from his people. He must have felt like "a fish out of the waters" of the Nile, somehow both enslaved by the lifestyle of his adopted family and yet set apart from his own people and rejected by them (2:14). Moses lives as a man divided in the space between two worlds. He belongs to neither the Hebrews nor the Egyptians and is shunned by both until, after trying to identify with the suffering of his people, he kills an Egyptian overseer. Moses' act is reported to the Egyptians by a Hebrew, and Moses flees into the wilderness.

It is in the wilderness that Moses finds security with an alternative family; he lives in permanent exile in the obscure hill country of Midian outside Pharaoh's control. For forty years Moses recovers. Each day he leads the sheep to graze in the scrubby wilderness. And although he may have passed a particular bush before and never given it a second glance, one day he imagines he sees flames licking its branches.

He might have wondered, as we might, what kind of fire burns but does not consume, what fire can be "living"—the fire burns, but not at the expense of the living bush. He might have asked himself what power or force works so differently from the way things usually work (for power or force usually acts *over against* something and seeks to destroy or to consume or to master). This fire is something new.

As Moses looks at the bush, something extraordinary happens. As Moses' attention and his curiosity draws him closer, God's new reality bursts in and changes Moses' life forever. God calls out his name: "'Moses ... I am the God of your father, the God of Abraham, the God of Isaac, and the God of Jacob'" (3:4–6).

This is no ordinary bush. And this is no ordinary trick, like the tricks Pharaoh's magicians performed. This is no ordinary voice of an ordinary, any old god either. Moses listens in surprise as God announces the history that Moses had forgotten. God evokes an old memory—one that is about to change the future. God comes straight to the point; there is work to be done:

> "I have observed the misery of my people who are in Egypt; I have heard their cry on account of their taskmasters. Indeed, I know their sufferings, and I have come down to deliver them from the Egyptians, and to bring them up out of that land to a good and broad land, a land flowing with milk and honey, to the country of the Canaanites .... I have also seen how the Egyptians oppress them. So come, I will send you to Pharaoh to bring my people, the Israelites, out of Egypt." (3:7–10)

God announces that new things are on the way. And from the very moment God speaks, the Hebrews receive a new name and a new identity. The people are no longer named because of their relationship *over against* the Egyptians or named by virtue of an earthly origin. (The word "Hebrew" might mean "from beyond the Euphrates" or refer to descendants of Eber, great grandson of Shem [Gen 10:21]). The people become Israelites: named from their relationship to God ("Israel" means "contending with God").

A familiar device? Moses' ancestors Abram and Jacob had been renamed (Gen 32:24–28; 35:10), but perhaps Moses had forgotten. For Moses, God's message spells disaster and the apparent unraveling of his new security. He had hoped himself well beyond such things, not just because of the awful prospect of being sent back to confront Pharaoh, but because Moses is unsure whether or not he actually counts as one of these new Israelites. He is thrown into panic as the past he thought he had escaped suddenly resurfaces. He squirms and wriggles:

> "Who am I that I should go to Pharaoh …? … Suppose they do not believe me or listen to me … I have never been eloquent, neither in the past nor even now that you have spoken to your servant; but I am slow of speech and slow of tongue. … Please send someone else." (Ex 3:11; 4:1, 10, 13)

And into Moses' mental anguish, into the freshly opened old wound of his divided self, God speaks:

> "I AM WHO I AM." … God also said to Moses, "Thus you shall say to the Israelites, 'The LORD, the God of your ancestors, the God of Abraham, the God of Isaac, and the God of Jacob, has sent me to you': This is my name forever, and this is my title for all generations." (3:14–15)

Moses hears the name that no mortal has ever heard before, and there is no response other than obedience. And so, despite a few more halfhearted grumbles, he sets off.

On his way back to Egypt, Moses must have relived painful memories as he explored his confused origins and divided loyalties. Perhaps it is in this light that we can read the curious incident in which God tries to harm Moses, seemingly because he is not circumcised as Israelite identity requires (4:24–26). While it is important to avoid making too much of this curious incident as Moses *walks the boundary* and *crosses over* the frontier between Midian and Egypt, this encounter with God recalls both the story of Jacob wrestling with God and acquiring a new name ("Israel" means "contending with God") and that of Abram's anxiety dream at Mamre. They are each stories about self-identity and about discovering a new identity in the midst of adversity.

Moses is rescued by the quick-thinking Zipporah who swiftly circumcises their son and then touches Moses' genitals with the foreskin. She reminds God of the covenant that binds God just as much as it binds the people thereby reframing Moses' relationship with God and reinstates his identity. With the covenant center stage in the narrative again, Moses is joined by Aaron and they go to the court of Pharaoh. Their mission is to confront the established imperial authority and state power with God's alternative reality.

Pharaoh and the plagues

The story of the plagues is drawn out over eight long chapters (Ex 5:1—12:36). Close scrutiny reveals a psychology of totalitarian control.

I do not recognize your right to negotiate with me. (5:1–23)

Moses and Aaron confront Pharaoh: the God of the *Israelites* says "'Let my people go, so that they may celebrate a festival to me'"

(5:1). But, asks Pharaoh, "'Who is the LORD, that I should heed him and let Israel go?'" (5:2) Who are these Israelites? Who is this God? What is this power other than my own? Pharaoh, ruler of this most powerful nation, has never heard of this people or their God. According to Pharaoh, "since we know everything there is to know," they can't possibly exist! Does that sound at all familiar to us?

Moses and Aaron try again, in language Pharaoh understands: "'The God of the *Hebrews*'" (5:3) says. Ah! Those Hebrew slaves! Have they got so little to do that they can contemplate taking time out? So Pharaoh increases their labor, and the Hebrew taskmasters who do the Egyptians' dirty work complain bitterly to Moses and Aaron who in turn complain to God.

Let the sanctions begin. (6:1–7:7)

God promised signs and wonders and great acts of judgment so that the people might believe. The Egyptians soon come to know who exactly this God of the Israelites is.

Scene 1: The staff becomes a snake. Twice. (7:8–14)

God commands Moses to turn his staff into a snake before Pharaoh. The state ruler summons his imperial wise men, sorcerers, and magicians to do the same with their own technologies. And although Moses' snake consumes the others, Pharaoh is not impressed.

Scene 2: Water turns to blood. (7:15–25)

Moses turned the water of the Nile into blood and Pharaoh's magicians did the same. Pharaoh is unimpressed.

Scene 3: Frogs. (8:1–15)

Moses makes frogs appear and so do Pharaoh's magicians. This time, however, Pharaoh responds; he asks Moses to remove the frogs. After the frogs disappear, Pharaoh quickly changes his mind. After all, superpowers do not deal with terrorists.

Scene 4: Gnats. (8:16–19)

Moses and Aaron turn the dust of the land into swarms of gnats. Pharaoh's magicians can't do gnats and so reluctantly advise Pharaoh that this might be the hand of God. Pharaoh ignores them, of course, and presumably the gnats, too, but he is starting to think.

Scene 5: Flies. (8:20–30)

Pharaoh goes for an early morning swim to get away from the gnats. Moses threatens him with flies. Flies everywhere, except in Goshem where the Israelites live. Away from his officials Pharaoh appears to concede: "'Go and sacrifice to your God within the land'" (8:25). Moses refuses. The Israelites need to go out into the desert. "OK," says Pharaoh, "Go, but not very far." And, he adds: "'Pray for me'" (8:28). Even as he reluctantly permits Moses' request, Pharaoh still demands some recognition of his own status. Needless to say, Pharaoh changes his mind as the last fly drops dead.

Scene 6: The Egyptians' livestock is struck with pestilence. (9:1–7)

This plague also distinguishes between Egyptians and Israelites. The pestilence strikes only the livestock of the Egyptians, just as the plague of flies avoided Goshem where the Israelites lived. Still Pharaoh refuses to budge, despite the damage to the national economy.

Scene 7: Boils from soot thrown up in the air. (9:8–12)

"The magicians could not stand before Moses because of the boils." (9:11). When Pharaoh refuses Moses' request again, these state officials begin to murmur their dissent.

Scene 8: Hail. Except in Goshem. (9:13–35)

God commands Moses to pay an early call on Pharaoh—before he had even donned his robes of state: "Tell him this time it's going to get personal—for you and your officials." The officials overhear

Moses and, for the first time, the machinery of the state stalls. Those officials who had begun to recognize the real power of this God of the Israelites run off to get their slaves and cattle under cover. Self-interest causes the bureaucratic apparatus to buckle. Now Pharaoh is obliged to acknowledge the reality of the Israelites' God. Pharaoh makes an extraordinary admission, using the very name of God: "'The LORD is in the right, and I and my people are in the wrong. ... I will let you go'" (9:28). Yet notice how he still believes he is able to negotiate with God and to change his mind when the hail melts away.

Scene 9: Locusts that eat away at what resistance remains. (10:1–20)

Moses and Aaron give notice to Pharaoh that God is by no means done. They warn Pharaoh that locusts are on the way unless he lets God's people go. This time Pharaoh's officials try to intervene: "'Let the people go ... do you not yet understand that Egypt is ruined?'" (10:7). For a while, this intervention seems to have the desired effect. Moses and Aaron are recalled and Pharaoh decides on damage limitation. He tries to negotiate the best deal he can: "'Which ones are to go?'" (10:8). Pharaoh wants only the men to go, not the children—his future slave force. Pharaoh is immovable on this point, so down come the locusts and consume the whole country. Moses and Aaron are recalled to Pharaoh's presence: "'I have sinned. ... forgive my sin. ... Pray to the LORD your God that at the least he remove this deadly thing from me'" (10:16–17). After the last locust vanishes once again Pharaoh decides to change his mind.

Scene 10: I give in. Get out of Egypt ... but not the cattle! (10:21–29)

Deep darkness falls across the land. Silence. No one moves. The machinery of the state is paralyzed. Except in Goshem.

Pharaoh decides he is ready for negotiation. He is prepared to let the Israelites go with their children, but not with their cattle. After all, they are his cattle and his flocks and his herds; after all, is he not Pharaoh, lord of all? When Moses refuses, Pharaoh hardens his heart once more; Pharaoh is used to having the final word.

Scene 11: One final dreadful deed. And capitulation? (11:1—12:36)

God decides that there is one final scene to act out, so God tells Moses to prepare the people. In the clearest of terms, Moses is to make sure that they are completely distinguishable from the Egyptians because the LORD will go through the land and " 'Every firstborn of the land of Egypt shall die,' " cattle and people (11:5).

God directs Moses and the people to make a sacrifice and mark their doorposts with the blood of a lamb they have killed and consumed. This historic act distinguishes them forever from other people and nations. "At midnight the LORD struck down all the firstborn in the land of Egypt …" (12:29). Pharaoh's power over his former slaves is broken forever and, as the Israelites leave, Pharaoh calls after them, begging a blessing from their God (12:32). Moses' long struggle with Pharaoh seems to be over at last, but we know that Pharaoh has one last move. As the Israelites rush out into the desert, Pharaoh, his eyes opened to the harsh reality of life without his slave workforce, readies himself for his final, futile gesture of military might and ignominy in the Red Sea.

The plague story as a mirror

The story of the plagues is an extraordinary part of the Exodus narrative. Not only is it a tale of struggle and eventual triumph, it is also an intriguing representation that mirrors other struggles. It mirrors the struggles that many small nations and minority interest groups experience today when they negotiate with major economic institutions, multinational and trans-global corporations, superpowers, and world authorities. On the face of it, Pharaoh entered the narrative as the absolute ruler of a totalitarian empire; he was the global power of his time. He had immeasurable resources of wealth, knowledge and technology, unchallengeable power, and life-and-death control over the large slave labor population upon which the success of his dominion was built. Like every superpower since, the Egyptian empire believed that it possessed all things supremely. There was nothing outside it, beyond it, or above it. Egypt was complete, self-contained excellence: the pinnacle of human history. And, like all totalitarian rulers, Pharaoh believed that there was simply no alternative to his rule and his regime. He did not need to heed the demands of Moses and his God.

But of course the climax here, the departure of the Israelites, is not the endpoint of Moses' mission. God called Moses, but not in order to wantonly defeat and humiliate the Egyptians. From God's perspective, the Egyptians are God's people, too, made in the image of the God whose fire burns without consuming. At the heart of this story is a message about God's judgment on the use of power, about Egypt's conduct as a superpower, about the structures of the Egyptian state and the nature of the leadership responsible for creating an economy and a culture based on slavery, brutality, control, and exploitation. Moses spoke out against Pharaoh's rule, his abuse of power, and his one-sided arbitrary laws, but the climax of the story is that God called the Israelites out of slavery and then proclaimed a new reality: God's alternative rule and Law.

This radically different reality is one that the Israelites would become acquainted with during their decades-long wandering in the wilderness. This reality would gradually form them into a nation with an alternative social order and a new and innovative community ethic based on what it means to live a just human life both under God and among equals. Those who once knew only the clenched hand and the *force of power used against them* are invited to learn how to *use power for others*. Those who were once slaves are to be set free to build an inclusive community of justice in and for the world. Those who were constrained by exploitation are soon to explore the experience of covenantal relationship in action, rooted in the momentous events on Mount Sinai.

The gift of the Law

The account of giving the Ten Commandments to Moses is well-known (Ex 20:1–21; Deut 5:1–22). Even if most people cannot actually remember all the commandments, the commandments' historic impact on the nature of moral discourse and social order has been extraordinary. The commandments articulate, not just a timeless vision for a radical egalitarian community, but also a functional model for its implementation.

The alternative nature of the Law does not, however, spring entirely unannounced at this precise moment in the Mosaic narrative. At various earlier points, the ground had already been prepared by references to God discriminating or distinguishing between the land of Goshem and the rest of Egypt, between the Israelites and the Egyptians (Ex 9:4, 26). God ensures that the Israelites are completely differentiated from the Egyptians for several days before the night of the Passover itself (11:7). Once at Sinai, where Moses receives the Law, the mountain is clearly demarcated as a "holy place," set apart from the people because of God's presence (19:12). In addition the Israelites are to be "marked out" from the other peoples (33:16) by virtue of their consecration to God. What was being forged was an identity based on "separation from" and "division between," a distinction that is later described as "clean" and "unclean."

Israel is to be a nation unlike other nations because they made the radical discovery of a God unlike any other god. And it is surely significant that God chose Moses, a man with a divided identity, to lead the Israelites out of exile and captivity, literally—out of *alien-nation*—towards wholeness. Like Moses, the Israelites go through the necessary wilderness process of rediscovering their identity under God before they can enter the Promised Land. It is ironic that Moses died in exile, divided finally and forever from his people (Deut 32:48–52). He never knew how the Israelites' new identity, with its new Law, fared after they left the wilderness and settled in Canaan.

Time to think about your own experience

In a time of silence you may now wish to consider your answers to the following questions. If you are with others in a group you may choose to share your responses with them.

- When have you felt bound or imprisoned by something and longed for an alternative? What were your alternatives? What might you take from the stories in Exodus to use in your prayer for an alternative future?

- When have you felt completely unable to make a difference in a situation? What stories do you know about ordinary women and men who have tried to make a difference in your local community? Are there any similarities between their stories and that of Moses and Aaron?

- How do the Ten Commandments (Ex 20:1–17; Deut 5:1–22) and the other laws (Ex 21—31) offer a radical alternative to the values of today's world?

■ Do you feel that God is more concerned that you change
   the world or that you save your soul? Are these the same
   thing? To what extent should people of faith who work for
   governments and major businesses involve themselves in
   the structures, activities, and values of their organizations
   and in world affairs?

Law, Risk, and Freedom:
Getting on the Inside of the Relationship

Few of us ever give much thought to the fact that the
Egyptians were made in the image of God and that the
Israelites' hasty exodus from the country must inevitably have
come as a terrible blow to ordinary Egyptians. For although the
Egyptians were no doubt implicated in, and presumably also
profiting from, an economy based on the exploitation of a slave
class, they nevertheless also lost goods, crops, cattle, and
firstborn infants.

Be this as it may, the clear message from the story of the
plagues is that God is quite capable of decisive action in order to
restore justice to those who suffer abusive rule. In the Bible we
learn repeatedly that God overturns self-satisfied, power-hungry
regimes and systems by acts of an unexpectedly radical nature.
This reality appears forgotten in the secular West, where we were
(until the recent terror attacks) comfortable in our sense of
domination and the security achieved through military might and
technology. It also appears forgotten by the declining church that
prefers to preoccupy itself with second- and third-order issues

instead of proclaiming justice, truth, and mercy amongst the powerful of the world.

The story of Moses reveals what happens when God decides to speak truth to power. The events at Sinai witness God's opening up of an alternative social order, of a radically innovative ethic based on justice and equality. It is an order that requires a diffusion of power throughout the community and is an experience of covenantal relationship in action. In short, the story of Moses is about the building of an inclusive community under the rule of God.

Now the particular rule of law in question here—the Law, Torah, or teaching given to the Israelites—is not the only moral system that has been given "directly" by God or mediated through some human agency. It is easy to cite other legal systems and to recognize that the range of possible ethical codes is limited only by particular histories and cultures.

But while people explore the possibility of creating a universal human moral code that might help in the evolution of dialogue, accord, and cooperation between different faiths and differing secular notions of morality, there is also a fundamental problem with moral systems that are rooted in particular religious texts or divine provenances. Religious texts often use their laws to perpetuate their own authority or to deny the integration of those considered "outsiders" into their communities or even to prevent the flourishing of these "outsider" groups or individuals.

Law as the path to life or the path to punishment?

The Law given by God on Sinai gives the Israelites a much-needed sense of identity. The Law also proposes the possibility of a radically different social ethic based on God's covenant. It is a system that articulates the importance of the Sabbath rest and ensures the stability of community life by honoring parents and forbidding murder, adultery, theft, lying, and covetousness. The

Law gives fundamental structure to an alternative egalitarian vision (Ex 20:8–17). And the Law begins with, and is rooted in, the declaration that there is only one God, that the Israelites shall worship no other god, and that this God is "a jealous God," fully prepared to punish or bless, depending on the ability of the people to keep faith and avoid the misuse of God's holy name (20:1–7).

Now if we believe that the One God is *wholly different* from any other god (so completely different that God could never be in the category of "one god among many gods," so different as to be the God-whose-fire-burns-without-consuming), then why does the text read that failure to worship God will cause God to punish "… to the third and the fourth generation of those who reject me, but showing steadfast love to the thousandth generation of those who love me and keep my commandments" (20:5–6)?

And why in Deuteronomy 30, on the giving of the Law, does God offer the path to life, on the one hand, and then threaten to punish those who fail to keep to that path?

> See, I have set before you today life and prosperity, death and adversity. If you obey the commandments of the LORD your God … by loving the LORD your God, walking in his ways, and observing his commandments, decrees, and ordinances, then you shall live and become numerous, and the LORD your God will bless you …. But if your heart turns away and you do not hear, but are led astray to bow down to other gods and serve them … you shall not live long in the land …. I call heaven and earth to witness against you today that I have set before you life and death, blessings and curses. Choose life so that you and your descendants may live. (30:15–19)

The Law itself seems to enshrine a basic anxiety about whether or not people will actually opt for life and choose to keep the commandments. Does God need to succumb to being "a god like other gods" and use coercive techniques in order to encourage the people to obey? And if God has to punish in order to elicit obedience, then how is God and the way God uses power any different from the regime from which the Israelites fled?

The problem of insiders and outsiders

The Jewish Law is no more problematic than any other ethical system. There is a fundamental problem with all systems that see good and bad as mutually self-referential and interdependent: "I only know that I am good or loved because I know, am told, or can see that you, or they, are bad and not loved." There is something wrong with notions of good and bad when they depend or require use against other people, when "good behavior" merits blessing and the restraint of punishment and "bad behavior" demands the punishment "from God's hand"— a reward or punishment *that the system itself* enshrines, permits, and commends.

Such systems harbor violence within themselves, a violence that is ready at any moment to be unleashed on those who fail to attain the standards of the Law. Such systems are disordered and pathological. They create identity by exclusion; they make "insiders" by virtue of identifying "outsiders." Such systems benefit the "chosen and elect" at the expense of the "despised and rejected." Such systems are not of God; they have nothing to do with the God whose-fire-burns-without-consuming and who does not use power in an arbitrary or abusive manner. Whether or not a system is based on divine revelation, the interpretation of a religious text, or is the product of a secular philosophy or sociopolitical group, a system that shapes group identity and values by exclusion and discrimination, enforced segregation, violent oppression, or exploitation cannot be allowed to stand unchallenged.

As I indicated in an article written for *Franciscan* magazine, it is likely that there have always been binary divisions within all societies: separation between those on the inside of power structures—the social elites—and those on the outside: "us and them," "haves and have-nots," "good and bad," "elect and damned," "sacred and profane."

In today's society the main binary division is based on gender. Male dominance still survives despite its gradual erosion by the challenge of feminist and other "minority" groups. Male dominance is reinforced by the traditional hegemony of white supremacy and Western secular educational values. This dominance effectively ensures the exclusion of a whole spectrum of people who may be classed as "outsiders" to suit the needs and purposes of the controlling elites.

Perhaps there is hallowed law in every world, justified as "divine decree," or the "will of the collective," or the "bidding of the leader." (The main binary division within Viking society, for instance, was between able-bodied men on the "inside" and, on the "outside," all non-fighting men, women and other "socially useless types." The one group had prestige, power, and control of the direction of the law; the other served the needs of the elite and was dependent upon them for their identity and access to social benefits.) Perhaps such binary divisions will always be the way human society is or perhaps it is just a lack of imagination.

Paul's vision of no division

Paul addressed the issue of binary division through male dominance. Although speaking of the Jewish Law through the lens of his newfound faith in Jesus Christ, nevertheless he articulates the possibility of an imaginative alternative practice. In Galatians

3, he places faith in Christ over against living by the law (3:23–25) and argues that life "in Christ"—being "baptized into Christ" (3:26–27)—impacts us not just individually but also as a community of believers. "There is no longer Jew or Greek, there is no longer slave or free, there is no longer male and female; for all of you are one in Christ" (3:28).

Paul suggests that the essential binary divisions of his day will dissolve for anyone opting to live the Christian life. He says that all believers are equal as "heirs according to the promise" (3:29). The implication is that those who choose to support or to maintain social division by race, status, or gender still live "according to the flesh" and are not fully living "in Christ" where there is no functioning or symbolic binary division. Paul wonders what "baptized into Christ" means for individuals and communities if not a meaningful change from a life of division that results in exploitation, inequality, and the abuse of power. Is not baptism a change from a life that reinforces the political and economic status quo, the prevailing social norms and unquestioned practices of exclusion, to a life in which essential social divisions are dissolved? Through baptism aren't all believers, whatever their race, social status, or gender, affirmed fully, inclusively, and effectively as representative of human personhood? (Biddington 3, 7)

For Paul and for those who opt for the fundamentally different priorities of life within the Body of Christ, faith in Jesus Christ means the ineluctable dissolution of harmful social division. Paul's egalitarian vision has, unfortunately, not prevented some who claim to share this vision from expressing their identity over against (and at the expense of) the Jewish Law and its adherents. It is common to hear sentiments such as: "I am a Christian and as such, I am in some way superior to others because I believe that Jesus' death on the cross 'abolished' the Law, which was, in any case, incapable of actually 'saving' anyone as I am saved."

God and the Law

This mistaken and unbiblical attitude signally fails to recognize that God is completely committed to the Law and all it represents. At the same time, God is immeasurably greater than the Law and is both able and willing to work through it and to radically reinterpret it in order to arrive at some new place and new understanding. This extraordinary reality is evident in Jeremiah; God chooses to ignore the covenant, to "suspend" the demands of the Law and to create an alternative response.

In Jeremiah 3:1–4:2 God laments that Israel is unfaithful to the covenant. Israel has run off with other gods and has become like a wife who turns prostitute, flouting all that was precious and special in their relationship. Jeremiah begins by having God quote part of the Law of Moses (Deut 24:1–4), which makes God's rights in the case quite clear:

> If a man divorces his wife
>   and she goes from him
> and becomes another man's wife,
>   will he return to her?
> Would not such a land be greatly polluted?
> You have played the whore with many lovers;
>   and would you return to me?
>   says the LORD. (Jer 3:1)

The Law states that there is no possibility for such a woman ever to return to her husband. It would be a calumny, a travesty of everything decent, of everything for which the Law stands. God repeats over and over that the Law is the Law and that such behavior has put Israel wholly outside the Law and deserving of the prescribed punishment. God is in a state of frenzied, abject indignation, ready to strike: "By the waysides you have sat waiting for lovers .... You have the forehead of a whore, you refuse to be ashamed" (3:2–3). But then out of the blue God announces something extraordinary, something utterly new and unforeseen that confounds all expectations:

> Return, faithless Israel ...
> I will not look on you in anger ... (3:11)

> Return, O faithless children ...
> > for I am your master ...
> > and I will bring you to Zion. (3:14)

> Return, O faithless children,
> > I will heal your faithlessness. (3:22)

> If you return, O Israel ...
> > if you return to me ...
> > then nations shall be blessed. (4:1–2)

Astonishing! God takes up the Law like a baker picks up a batch of dough. God twists it and stretches it and makes of it something that Moses could never have imagined. God reinterprets the Law and recreates it *for the sake of the covenant relationship.* At the very point at which Israel committed an act that spelled "The End," an act that would oblige God to respond with punishment and destruction, at the very moment when the Law appears ready to implode, forcing God to become just "a god amongst other gods," God calls the people to a new place, a place where something is disclosed that is more important than the Law. God reveals something new; God unveils the "yet-more" about God. And an extraordinary new dimension to the relationship between God and humankind is created.

This invitation to walk with God into a new place and to develop a relationship of mutuality has a "givenness" about it. The Law is nonnegotiable, and yet God disclosed the "something more." And this disclosure of new possibility, this revelation of an unconditional openness to what might be, *cannot be taken back or erased.* For God's invitation is part of our Scripture. The invitation is there in black and white, and it allows us to see that God is always more than we anticipate. God is always at work on that "dangerous edge of things," when catastrophe threatens and where only venturesome love can engage creatively with each successive opportunity and risk.

Jesus as a risk taker

Jesus lived in the creative tension between fulfilling established messianic expectations and pursuing the risk-shaped demands of venturesome love. His destiny was to live on this painful knife-edge by turning the Law—the religious life—from something safe, predictable, and exclusive into something radically different, thoroughly inclusive, and distinctly subversive. And this mission inevitably brought him into conflict with the Pharisees, who felt they lived the Law in a creative and challenging way.

The Pharisees took it upon themselves to keep the entirety of the Law—something only formally required of the priestly class. The Pharisees believed that the Law was meant for all Jews, that living it to the full was an expression, not only of their commitment to the covenant, but also of a means to assert their identity. Their religious observance was a power, a subversive defiance against the occupying forces of Rome, much as militant or fundamentalist expressions of faith often emerge in response to oppression by foreign powers or exploitation by economic forces. Jesus was clearly close to the Pharisees; he often attended their regular Sabbath meals after Friday worship. But he also questioned their understanding of the Law and their effectiveness in using it to express the truth that God's power is altogether different from human power.

Witness, for instance, that Sabbath day in the cornfields (Mk 2:23–28) when the hungry disciples pick the ears of corn. The Pharisees comment that Sabbath work is proscribed by the Law. Jesus responds that the Law can be put aside at times of need, that it can be broken, that King David broke the Law, and that " 'The sabbath was made for humankind, and not humankind for the sabbath' " (2:27).

A new Law

Jesus repeatedly asks people to consider interpreting the Law in a new way, a way that turns the Law's conventions inside out and upside down. Jesus frees us to discover that we no longer need the insider-outsider dichotomy that characterizes and perpetuates the *over against* identity of the Law. We no longer need the disciplines of power that reduce the Law to just another ethical system and God to just another god.

Jesus presents an alternative reading of the Law throughout his earthly ministry, and in particular in that curious ten-verse re-presentation of the Ten Commandments known as the Sermon on the Mount:

"Blessed are the poor in spirit, for theirs is the kingdom of heaven.
"Blessed are those who mourn, for they will be comforted.
"Blessed are the meek, for they will inherit the earth.
"Blessed are those who hunger and thirst for righteousness, for they will be filled.
"Blessed are the merciful, for they will receive mercy.
"Blessed are the pure in heart, for they will see God.

"Blessed are the peacemakers, for they will be called
children of God.
"Blessed are those who are persecuted for righteousness'
sake, for theirs is the kingdom of heaven.
"Blessed are you when people revile you and persecute you
and utter all kinds of evil against you falsely on my
account. Rejoice and be glad, for your reward is great in
heaven, for in the same way they persecuted the prophets
who were before you." (Mt 5:3–12)

During his ministry people frequently asked Jesus for his ruling
on a particular issue; and his response was typically to tell a story
or parable, a method entirely in keeping with the approach of any
rabbi. Matthew, whose Gospel portrays Jesus as the new Moses,
offers the Beatitudes as a New Testament response to—and
equivalent of—the Ten Commandments.

Although the Beatitudes are not a concrete, complete moral
system, they present an imaginative vision based on a radically
alternative approach to belonging, identity, and power. This
alternative vision proceeds, neither by separating off those who fail
to live up to the group behavior ("You shall not ...."), nor by
threatening to unloose the proscribed wrath ("You shall not ...."
Or else!). Instead the Beatitudes invite individuals to *identify
themselves* as "those who hunger ... those who mourn ... those who
are peacemakers," and to thereby *include themselves* in a community
that God is passionate about, cares for, values, and blesses. Indeed,
this beatific vision reveals God's preference is for the poor and
those who identify with the poor and is set against only those who
cause suffering, persecution, and mourning.

The Beatitudes offer an alternative vision that is radically
inclusive. There is no "in-betweenness"—to use Arendt's phrase—
that separates "them" from "others", no inherent division between

"insider" and "outsider." An individual has to deliberately choose to be an outsider by distancing him or her self from those who suffer: "I am not in any sense hungry, nor in mourning, nor persecuted." Moreover this vision enshrines the presence of God at the creative (and therefore the dangerous) edge of life, that unexpected moment when "I may come to know hunger, loss, or persecution, and so might also come to experience God." The Beatitudes offer a vision that is necessarily open to the future, to the what-might-be, to the "yet more" of God. And by assenting to an openness to the future, this vision is one that is also likely to draw people to "the inside" of a relationship with God.

Getting on the inside of God

Being "on the inside" of a relationship with God means to be in a place beyond the insider-outsider dichotomy—for no one is outside of God, except as the result of a deliberate choice. Being on the inside of such a relationship is, therefore, to be in a place characterized by an unceasing invitation to participate freely in divine creativity and to discover a freeing mutuality between humanity and divinity. This mutuality allows us to be loved and embraced within the re-creative and regenerative power of God, and so become like God—even in our human flesh. Being on the inside means to be enabled by God's power to overcome division and anxiety, to be enabled to conceive and concede that death and deathliness are not all-powerful, and so to imagine and birth God's fresh beginnings and radical newness. Finally, being in such a place means to articulate, ever more boldly, that "being-toward-life" really does condition everything. And this revelation demands that human flourishing, the nurturing of all life, and the creation of inclusive communities of blessing, is the real vocation to which God calls us.

To be on the inside of a relationship with God, however, is also to be in a place which we are bound to flee, because to know and share God's re-creative power is also to know God's voice. To hear this voice is to experience at firsthand God's creative speech and so be compelled to unbind God from the tomb into which we have allowed God to be buried.

Time to think about your own experience

In a time of silence you may now wish to consider your answers to the following questions. If you are with others in a group you may choose to share your responses with them.

- When and where have you noticed someone who has been excluded from a group, a community, or a church? How do the dynamics of exclusion work? Does God ever work to exclude people? What could you do to include those on the outside?

- Because God never coerces people or resorts to threats or force, what should the priorities of your discipleship and the mission of your church be within your local community?

- Compare the Ten Commandments (Ex 20:1–17) with the Beatitudes (Mt 5:3–11). How do they each work as a system that discloses or reveals the true nature of God? Which best resonates with your experience of the life of faith and discipleship? Can you prefer or value one faith without feeling superior to those who prefer another?

- Try to imagine being "on the inside" of a relationship with God. What might it mean? What is it like? What difference might it make to who you are? How might it enrich what it means to be a disciple or a Christian?

Jeremiah: On Defying the Ways that Lead to Death

Jeremiah was "son of Hilkiah, of the priests who were in Anathoth in the land of Benjamin" (Jer 1:1). Jeremiah comes, as Walter Brueggemann reminds us, from the outside, from a nowhere sort of place. Anathoth is famous for nothing *except* for being the place where King Solomon banished Abiathar (his father David's high priest) after Abiathar attempted an uprising against Solomon when he came to the throne (1 Kgs 2:26) (Brueggemann 30). Jeremiah comes from Anathoth, from way outside the political establishment of the ruling elite; he was descendant of an exiled priestly troublemaker. Jeremiah's call is like a symbolic return of the old traditions and practices of the Exodus and the wilderness. It is as though the voice of Moses himself—silenced from the moment Solomon came to power and set about creating a different regime—is heard again through Jeremiah.

Jeremiah's call

The proclamation of a radical new way to be in the world, which was the task of Moses, is handed on to Jeremiah. And Jeremiah, despite his own deep reservations, is called to speak out against the religious and political establishment of his day:

> Then I said, "Ah, Lord GOD! Truly I do not know how to speak, for I am only a boy." But the LORD said to me,
> "Do not say, 'I am only a boy';
> for you shall go to all to whom I send you,

> and you shall speak whatever I command you,
> Do not be afraid of them,
> for I am with you to deliver you, says the LORD."
> Then the LORD ... touched my mouth; and ... said to me,
> "Now I have put my words in your mouth.
> See, today I appoint you over nations and over
>   kingdoms,
> to pluck up and to pull down,
> to destroy and to overthrow,
> to build and to plant." (Jer 1:6–10)

Jeremiah stands in a long tradition of interlopers from the margins who are used in significant ways by God. Think not only of Moses, the confused foster child in a foreign land, but also of the anxious wanderer Abraham before him, and Jesus himself from the equally nowhere place of Nazareth. The word of God comes to Jeremiah for those at the center of the political and religious life of Judah. His task is to speak the truth to the leaders of the established religion, shatter their complacency, and compel them to recognize how God's future differs from what they imagined it to be.

Jeremiah's situation

During the early part of Jeremiah's life, King Josiah reigned in Judah. He made an attempt to be faithful to the covenant and to abolish idolatrous practices. One of Josiah's efforts was to repair the temple. In the course of the repair workers discovered what was believed to be a copy of the long-lost Torah. This Torah was read aloud, and Josiah led the people in a great act of national repentance and a celebration of the Passover. Unfortunately, Josiah was killed in battle against the Egyptians and was succeeded by each of his sons in turn. The first two sons were puppets, put on the throne by Pharaoh. The last son, Zedekiah, was installed by Nebuchadnezzar, the king of Babylon. Zedekiah returned Judah to the old idolatrous practices that existed before his father Josiah's reign. He undid his father's reforms and the nation's rededication to the Torah. By 597 BCE the nation was in political chaos. The Babylonians had captured Jerusalem. Nebuchadnezzar levied a heavy tribute, sacked the temple, and deported many of the leading inhabitants of Jerusalem to Babylon. Despite this chaos, both Zedekiah and Hananiah (the official prophet of the royal establishment and its cult) were convinced that Jerusalem was the safest place to be because it was the location of the temple. The two men mistakenly believed that the temple guaranteed both God's abiding presence in the land and the covenant made to David and his descendants.

Although Zedekiah and Hananiah believed that Jerusalem was inviolable, secure, and protected by God, they both failed to read the signs of the times. They thought that an uncritical adherence to the ritual practices of the covenant would solve all their security fears and that the community (or what remained of it) was in a good, healthy condition because of its faithful ritual observance. Both king and priest mistakenly believed that the temple and its rituals would enable the nation to resist the threat of its enemies; that the occupation they experienced was just a temporary upset and rectifiable by a new allegiance with their former enemy, Egypt.

Jeremiah's message

Jeremiah preached in the context of this daily denial of reality: life lived under foreign domination. Through Jeremiah God warned both religious and political leaders against an easy reliance on the established rituals, wisdom, and traditions they erroneously thought would keep them secure. Indeed, God gave due notice to

the inhabitants of Jerusalem and the fortified cities, the
circumcised and uncircumcised, Israelite and non-Israelite alike:

> Thus says the LORD: Do not let the wise boast in their
> wisdom, do not let the mighty boast in their might, do not
> let the wealthy boast in their wealth; but let those who boast
> boast in this, that they understand and know me, that I am
> the LORD; I act with steadfast love, justice, and righteousness
> in the earth, for in these things I delight, says the LORD.

> The days are surely coming … when I will attend to all
> those who are circumcised only in the foreskin: Egypt,
> Judah, Edom, the Ammonites, Moab, and all those with
> shaven temples who live in the desert. For all these nations
> are uncircumcised, and all the house of Israel is
> uncircumcised in heart. (Jer 9:23–26)

God warned repeatedly of impending judgment, but no one
listened. God spoke of breaking down and plucking up the cities
and the walls in which people trusted, of "bringing disaster on all
flesh," and God promised that those who dwelt in the cities would
be lucky to escape with their lives.

Jeremiah and Hananiah

In an extraordinary encounter, the priest Hananiah finds
Jeremiah prophesying one day in the temple before all the other
priests and representatives of the establishment. This encounter
becomes a kind of "showdown" between the establishment figure,
Hananiah, and Jeremiah, the outsider and descendant of
troublemakers and traitors. In the hearing of all his people
Hananiah announces to Jeremiah that he, Hananiah, has been told
by God that normality will soon be restored:

"Thus says the LORD of hosts, the God of Israel: I have broken the yoke of the king of Babylon. Within two years I will bring back to this place all the vessels of the LORD's house, which King Nebuchadnezzar of Babylon took away from this place .... I will also bring back to this place King Jeconiah son of Jehoiakim of Judah ... who went to Babylon." (Jer 28:2–4a)

Hananiah is confident that, through the ongoing negotiations with the Egyptians, God will have things back to normal within two years at the most. Jeremiah replies: "Amen! May the LORD do so; may the LORD fulfill the words that you have prophesied" (28:6). Who could not wish that to happen? But then he adds words that cause Hananiah to wince, words that give the lie to his ability to know and to speak anything authentic from God:

"But listen now to this word that I speak ... in the hearing of all the people. The prophets who preceded you and me from ancient times prophesied war, famine, and pestilence against many countries and great kingdoms. As for the prophet who prophesies peace, when the word of that prophet comes true, then it will be known that the LORD has truly sent the prophet." (28:7–9)

The prophets of old never warned of good things. That is not what prophecy is about: "Good luck to you if you want to start a new tradition," Jeremiah seems to suggest, "but will it be of God?"

Hananiah responds to this affront by breaking the wooden ox's yoke that Jeremiah carried on his shoulders to symbolize the people's oppression. This act was more than an expression of his contempt for Jeremiah, more than symbolically implying that the yoke of Babylon would be thrown off within two years, Hananiah's act was an attempt to render Jeremiah powerless. And Hananiah appears to succeed, for Jeremiah retreats in silence. But before long, Jeremiah is back bearing a heavy iron yoke to symbolize that the people would serve their overlords even longer and harder than they imagined. The only thing that was true (albeit ironically) about Hananiah's prophecy was that within two years Hananiah himself would be dead:

> "Listen, Hananiah, the LORD has not sent you, and you made this people trust in a lie. Therefore thus says the LORD: I am going to send you off the face of the earth. Within this year you will be dead, because you have spoken rebellion against the LORD." (28:15–16)

The heart of Jeremiah's message is: "… you made this people trust in a lie … you have spoken rebellion against the LORD." The showdown was between the truth-telling outsider and the "spin doctor" of a corrupt and compromised regime, between two versions of who God is: the God who fits conveniently into political wrangling and wheeling-dealing or the God who is utterly unlike other gods, untamable, and utterly beyond any misguided attempts to make God subject to human direction.

Speaking the truth

Hananiah lied about the nation's plight and its causes. He lied about God to keep himself in power, either because he was not a real prophet or because he could not bring himself to speak a message that would upset the comfortable familiarity of his life. Jeremiah, on the other hand, is able to speak the truth. Jeremiah's call is to be the bearer of a profound countercultural message. Jeremiah's message is chiefly about God's unraveling of the familiar securities of life. But Jeremiah's message is also one of profound hope, for the God who unravels and brings things to nothing is also the God who is able to bring to life things that do not exist.

Jeremiah's God is *vital*, committed to life and to the people. And God's commitment and vitality demand both truth-telling from God and Jeremiah's obedience. To this end, God has Jeremiah write to those Israelites living in exile:

> Thus says the LORD of hosts … to all the exiles whom I
> have sent into exile from Jerusalem to Babylon: Build
> houses and live in them; plant gardens and eat what they
> produce. Take wives and have sons and daughters; …
> multiply there, and do not decrease. But seek the welfare
> of the city where I have sent you into exile, and pray to
> the LORD on its behalf, for in its welfare you will find your
> welfare. For thus says the LORD of hosts, the God of Israel:
> Do not let the prophets and the diviners who are among
> you deceive you, and do not listen to the dreams that they
> dream, for it is a lie that they are prophesying to you in my
> name; I did not send them. (Jer 29:4–9)

God's grief

As events continue, Jeremiah will once again find himself the bearer of God's unwelcome truth. For rather than inciting predictable resistance and urging the Israelites to be a thorn in the flesh of their hosts, he writes to the exiles that God bids them settle down and prosper. Common sense, no doubt. The people's security lay with that of their captors, but Jeremiah also knew that God was already at work. Even in exile the seeds of restoration were being sown, watered by God's own tears of grief:

> Thus says the LORD:
> We have heard a cry of panic,
>   of terror, and no peace. (Jer 30:5)

Do not be dismayed, O Israel. (30:10)

Your hurt is incurable,
    your wound is grievous.
There is ... no medicine for your wound,
    no healing for you. (30:12–13)

Why do you cry out over your hurt?
    Your pain is incurable. ...
    I have done these things to you. (30:15)

The destruction that befell the people, their removal into exile
from the land of promise, and their grief (and God's grief) become
the touchstone for God's breathtaking act of newness. At the very
moment when all seemed lost, at the very point of collapse, and in
the contemplation of permanent assimilation within the alien
culture of the Babylonians, God announces: "I will restore health
to you, and your wounds I will heal" (30:17).

Again God proves that, for the sake of their relationship, God
will overturn the people's anticipated future. But it is important to
recognize that this promised healing is no easy resolution—no cheap
grace—for either covenant partner. The people's restoration is a
spontaneous and creative outcome *that can only happen* after the
experience of mutual pain and sorrow on the far side of anguish.

The pain is articulated in the poetry of Chapter 31, which
anticipates the restoration of both the northern kingdom Israel
(31:1–22) and the southern kingdom Judah (31:23–26). From the
desert a wind blows over the silent ruins and, on the wind is heard
the sound of Rachel weeping for all that has been lost:

Thus says the LORD:
A voice is heard in Ramah,
    lamentation and bitter weeping.

Rachel is weeping for her children;
>   she refuses to be comforted ...
>   because they are no more. (31:15)

But God sees Rachel's tears and hears her cry. In a beautifully moving text, God expresses deep love and compassion for her and for Ephraim, the children of Israel:

Thus says the LORD:
>   Keep your voice from weeping,
>   and your eyes from tears;
for there is a reward for your work ...
>   they shall come back from the land of the enemy;
there is hope for your future ...
>   your children shall come back to their own country.
Indeed I heard Ephraim pleading:
"You disciplined me ...
>   I was like a calf untrained.
Bring me back, let me come back,
>   for you are the LORD my God.
For after I had turned away I repented;
>   and after I was discovered, I struck my thigh;
I was ashamed, and I was dismayed
>   because I bore the disgrace of my youth."
Is Ephraim my dear son?
>   Is he the child I delight in?
As often as I speak against him,
>   I still remember him.
Therefore I am deeply moved for him;
>   I will surely have mercy on him. (31:16–20)

Out of God's abiding love comes the promise that there will be a return from exile and that the most remarkable things will happen as God returns the people to their promised land:

> Set up road markers for yourself,
>   make yourself guideposts;
> consider well the high way,
>   the road by which you went.
> Return, O virgin Israel,
>   return to these your cities.
> How long will you waver,
>   O faithless daughter?
> For the LORD has created a new thing on the earth:
>   *a woman encompasses a man.* (31:21–22; emphasis
>   mine)

The exact nature of this "new thing" is uncertain. The verb "encompass" could mean "protect," "pay court to," "embrace," or "press round." It may suggest the idea of a woman triumphing over a man, or the notion of a woman taking the initiative in lovemaking, or even more remarkably, that Israel got the better of God and that God does not mind. Whatever the precise meaning, the strange idea of "a woman encompassing a man" is surely intended to represent the "yet-more" of God, the astonishing novelty, freshness, and vitality of the new life that God desires and the new order that will be birthed.

A new covenant

At the heart of Jeremiah's proclamation of profound renewal is God's burning desire for a radical social justice that will overcome the structures and behavior that promote death. Although Jeremiah is particularly scathing about the establishment and its politics, he is also critical of the religious attitudes and practices encouraged by institutional religion. The people are allowed to believe that God could be held to the Abrahamic covenant, renewed at the time of Moses, *simply by keeping the regulations* prescribed by the Law, that keeping the Law would be enough to guarantee both personal well-being and the security of the community. Jeremiah preaches that a radical concern for justice and equality is the real essence of the covenant. The original covenant, symbolized by the marking of flesh and blood and the observation of certain prohibitions, had patently failed. Now Jeremiah discloses that the covenant is to be restored through a new inner "covenantal state of being" marked by a *permanent and mutually re-creative covenant* between God and humankind:

> The days are surely coming, when I will make a new covenant with the house of Israel and the house of Judah. It will not be like the covenant that I made with their ancestors when I took them by the hand to bring them out of the land of Egypt—a covenant that they broke, though I was their husband [or master], says the LORD. But this is the covenant that I will make with the house of Israel after those days ... I will put my law within them, and I will write it on their hearts; and I will be their God, and they shall be my people. No longer shall they teach one another, or say to each other, "Know the LORD," for they shall all know me, from the least of them to the greatest ... for I will forgive their iniquity, and remember their sin no more. (Jer 31:31–34)

God promises that the people will be re-created and that a new inner nature will be given to them. Their nature will be rooted in—and born of—the knowledge that whatever happens, God will always forgive them. Out of the crisis wrought by the failure of the covenant and the resultant despair, God finds a new way to engage with the people: *to love them unconditionally.* Jeremiah articulates both God's newness at work in the face of assured annihilation, justly sanctioned by the Law, and the mutually re-creative nature of God's covenant, "For I will forgive their iniquity, and remember their sin no more." He reveals God's fundamental commitment to forgiveness, for God discloses a nature that is neither fixed, unchanging, nor unyielding. God is revealed as open, flexible, and responsive, and willing to enter into a relationship with the people that is henceforth reciprocal and open to change. The promise that God held out and that Jeremiah proclaimed to the remnant in Judah and to the exiles in Babylon has come true. And God's re-creative power flows freely again.

Because Jeremiah proclaimed God's message to a people in exile, Jeremiah can be compared with Moses, who gave the Law to the Israelites as they struggled in the wilderness. Both men offered a revelation from God that was birthed into exile, confusion, and disconnectedness. Both articulated a vision in which disorientation, anxiety, and loss of meaning become the occasion and opportunity for God to create new life from death and decay. The establishment failed to consider that it had ceased to follow the path to life. It was neither alert nor open to the possibility of unforeseen novelty and astonishing originality on the part of God. These are the failures that ultimately brought about the chaos and disaster. Jeremiah's message caused such a tremendous outrage that he was lucky to escape with his life.

One last detail remains to be considered. If Jeremiah the prophet were to write a letter to those of us who feel we live in exile in today's disoriented and fragmented world, what exactly would he say? And would we be open and brave enough to hear his message, to act and to change?

Time to think about your own experience

In a time of silence you may now wish to consider your answers to the following questions. If you are with others in a group you may choose to share your responses with them.

■ The prophet Hananiah was probably a good man and a patriot since he clearly believed God was calling him to ensure his country's stability in adverse circumstances. Jeremiah, on the other hand, could be seen as a rather unstable character, who believed that God wanted an end to the status quo. What do you think each would say about your church community?

■ Who are the prophets in your church? How do you listen to their voices? How important is social justice to your discipleship and faith? What role does the church play in ushering in radical newness?

■ When newcomers arrive at your church do people hope they won't interfere with the established routines, or do church members anticipate that the newcomers may offer fresh insights? How could you discover what response newcomers experience in your church?

■ What signs do you see that God is open to the future? Try to imagine how God might be found in each new event, change, or experience that has happened to you.

Is the Matrix Real?
On Being Born Afresh into Hope

The parallels between Jeremiah's time and that of our world
and church are not difficult to make. Contemporary Western
society suffers from an acute disorientation about its identity and
values. We Westerners seem to act almost as though we are
content to let everything implode and be brought to naught rather
than to admit we are seriously damaged and desperately craving
some shred of comfort and enchantment to heal our
disconnectedness.

In recent decades we have witnessed many attempts to satisfy
the deep desire for re-enchantment and reintegration through the
reassuring, anodyne "disneyfication" of our culture and the
runaway, spellbinding success of the magical worlds of Harry Potter
and *The Lord of the Rings* in which invincible superheroes save
humanity and always prevail over evil. Today we have exactly the
same need for security as the people of Jeremiah's day and the
same discourses of fear still reign free and seduce us into believing
that the only options open to us lead uncontrollably to the
hopelessness of death.

This fear is the real spell we are under. It is a spell that needs
"unspelling" and this can only be done by attending to the voice of
the One who "gives life to the dead." Jeremiah spoke critically to
the political and religious establishments of his day against the fear
that held them both enthralled. The question for us is whether or
not the church of our time is held tightly in the grip of the forces
of death that prevail in our society. Does fear disable the church

from speaking and organizing the radical hope that is its most
sacred message to proclaim? We may even find ourselves asking
whether a fascination with death actually blinds the church to the
urgent state of things thereby intimidating it into a preoccupation
with the unessential third-order issues while the world looks on in
need. Perhaps, too, we may wonder what Jeremiah would say if he
were to stand today outside a cathedral, as he once did outside the
temple in Jerusalem.

Learning from Jeremiah—and Hananiah

Given the Western church's massive decline, there is little
doubt that Jeremiah's message to our church today would be that it
is time to change or die. It is also likely that he would point out
that the church has not only lost the authoritative place in society
it once had, but also lacks any real ability to speak truth to the
matrix of immensely well-buttressed and self-perpetuating systems
and structures of power that currently prevail. He would say, too,
that the church is no longer able to speak effectively to people in
ways that impact their personal lives.

Is the church all over and done with? It is God's church, of
course, and God is ultimately in control—however terrifying or
frustrating that may feel. Perhaps what is happening is simply a
sign of God unsettling us and alerting us to those things that have
gone wrong. Perhaps God is penetrating our numbness and our
woeful lack of imagination as Jeremiah tried to do. It does certainly
appear that the church needs to change.

First and foremost, as a church we need to step away from our
fixation with the "ark mentality," that is, in stormy times like ours,
a knee-jerk response for security that turns the church into a place
with narrow doorways and no windows. For with narrow doorways
and no windows, we are unable to see where we are and where
God is leading us. (And without windows allowing the Spirit to

blow in, the stench inside can be overpowering!) We need be to open, to see what is outside, what is around us, and so to permit God to rouse us to the possibility of discovering new things, new voices, and bold new prophets. Like Hananiah, we may desperately desire to hold on to the same old things done in the same old ways. We need to learn that, whatever these new things might be, we can be sure they will spring from the utterly unimaginable newness that comes only from God, things God would give us and have us be, things we cannot yet conceive.

Opening ourselves to new understandings, attitudes, and practices is undeniably a painful process. And very often it feels as though the church has followed Hananiah's lead and opted to face the uncertainties of the future by taking refuge within a seemingly closed system of theological thought and practice. This theology is all about words from the past. Theological inquiry and theologically reflective pastoral practice appear to have become confined to ever shuffling the same pieces of simplistically interpreted revelation the way a child shuffles bricks to build a model church. Such an image begs the question of whether there is more than one means of interpreting Scripture and doing theology. Such an approach raises the possibility of whether there might be fresh ways of understanding what church might look like. If God's nature is to be open, flexible, and responsive and the relationship God has with people is reciprocal and open to change, then why can't the church, for instance, be bigger on the inside than it seems on the outside? Why does the church seem as little capable of transformation as any secular institution? What is holding the church back?

The church and authority

The question of authority is as central for the church today as it was for Jeremiah. Where is truth to be located and how is it to be authenticated? Whose version of the nature of God is trustworthy? How does God require us to be and act in the light of our understanding of God's nature?

The church has always claimed to have Jesus' authority to identify the ways that lead to life. Consequently the church has seen its role in the world as one of speaking truth to power, and of promoting a community life according to the radically different values of God's reign. Yet all too often the church has preferred "closedness" to "openness" and the "fixed completeness" of revelation instead of a belief that God is forever becoming, forever birthing, forever new.

Historically the church has not encouraged its members to find and respond to God in the provisional, in the coming-to-birth, or in the risky crisis moments of collapse and opportunity. Indeed, the church has modeled itself after the secular societies in which it has found itself, locating its power base in the weight of past tradition and precedent and rooting its authority and influence in the maintenance of the status quo. Yet the church could have modeled itself on the authority of a God whose power is like a fire-that-can-burn-without-harming-the-bush, a power that is not exercised at the expense of, or over against, someone or something else. The church could have chosen to be a sign of radically different understanding of the authority of God and thereby enabled its members to live as Jesus urged.

Where is the church's authority located?

Although we should never fall into the trap of thinking that God can only speak through the church, for there is plenty of evidence to the contrary, understandings of the church's authority has undergone a sea change in the twentieth century. The question of authority can be approached in two ways. On one hand, we may ask whether the church has the authority it needs to proclaim a fundamentally different approach to God and to human living. On the other hand, we might ask how might people be persuaded to give authority to the church, to take it seriously, and to listen long enough to hear and respond.

Theologian Rowan Williams, Archbishop of Canterbury, argues that the authority of the church is rooted in both its right to decide for itself what ideas and actions count as Christian (and, therefore presumably, where the boundaries lie) and also in its credibility with those who are inside as much as with those who are on the outside—since authority is both earned and given. As far as the church is concerned, Williams contends that its authority to speak is derived from its witness to Scripture, from its faithful following of the things Jesus asked be done "in memory of him," and from the expression of a belief in God who is active in the world (Williams 16–28).

The unequivocal respect that revealed truth held in the past has lost ground to the preference today for that which can be experienced and authentically verified by individuals and by communities in daily living. The underpinning of action by revealed truth, which was the linchpin of Christian identity, has been severely loosened by the contemporary appeal to experience. Consequently the church must seek to regain credibility by learning how to relocate its authority in its actions. It must learn how to respond afresh and inclusively to the pastoral needs of society by articulating and practicing the ways that lead to new life and flourishing. In this regard, it could do worse than look to the example of those many groups that exist to offer pastoral support and advocacy to those whom the church has excluded, meaning groups whose members' human experience frequently challenges the neat boundaries of the church's worldview by virtue of the "problematic" theological issues they bring, whether it be gender, sexual identity, marital status, or social marginalization.

Williams' concern is that the church's basic identity, speech, and action must be negotiated with strict reference to Scripture. And as far as the "world outside" is concerned, if the church wants to derive action from the revealed truth of the Bible, that is fine. The world is not really interested, and the reason has something to do with a perceived lack of honesty by and in the church about the ways Scripture may be interpreted. While there is always a patent problem about knowing exactly how to read texts in the particular context in which we happen to live, there is a *dis*-ease about the church's ready tendency to "safe," closed, one-dimensional readings that are so often used to justify exclusion and judgmentalism.

If we wish to encourage an effective and inclusive pastoral practice appropriate to the twenty-first century, we need to ask whether or not we can be satisfied any longer with routinely reciting, uncritically accepting, and mechanically regurgitating the same scriptural readings, theological formulae, and moral attitudes that have accrued over the centuries. Do we instead need to allow God to rescue us from those undemanding habits and from the obsession with fixedness and certainty that can so easily restrict God's novelty? Can we instead allow God to lead us to flourishing and fullness of life through our discovery of the "multi-layeredness" and "open-endedness" of the texts and the multivalency and plurality of their possible interpretations?

Creation, atonement, and new life

Creation itself may, for instance, be better understood, not as a one-off seven-day event, a closed system, complete and never-to-be-repeated, but as an ongoing process of unfolding from new birth to new birth, evolving over time, in which we participate and which reflects the nature of God and God's revelation. While this dynamic understanding of creation does justice both to the Hebrew text and to current state of scientific opinion, it also serves to raise questions about traditional interpretations of other related theological ideas.

For instance, if God is ever open and becoming, ever bringing new life to birth, ever receptive to the what-might-be, and if God leads us to understand creation as an open system, then how might the doctrine of atonement fare in the light of this understanding?

The theologian James Alison (himself someone whose sexual identity has put him at odds with the church) reminds us that atonement, like creation, is a process, a re-creative journey of self-discovery, a coming to faith *that needs to be first embodied and experienced before it can be articulated.* Atonement is not about the acceptance of Jesus-as-savior that requires mere intellectual assent without an actual change of lifestyle (Alison 28).

The first disciples themselves "discovered" atonement through their experience of Jesus at his resurrection and in their later reflection on his life, work, and teaching in the light of that resurrection. For them atonement and salvation *flowed from experiencing Jesus* to be "Lord and savior," and they subsequently remodeled their lives in the light of this experience. Their experience of wholeness in their lives was sufficient basis for their transformative new faith.

In a sense the move from prioritizing the transformative value of direct experience of Jesus to asserting "creedal" belief in Jesus was inevitable with the passage of time. And this change is visible in the New Testament itself. In Matthew's Gospel, for example, the disciples' exclamation of faith as Jesus calms the storm " 'Truly you are the Son of God' " (Mt 14:33) is based on their experience of him. But by the time John's Gospel was written the emphasis has shifted and the task was to enable people to "*come to believe* that Jesus is the Messiah, the Son of God, and that *through believing* you may have life in his name" (Jn 20:31, emphasis mine). Yet even these vicarious interpretations of the disciples' experience of the resurrected Jesus-as-savior differ markedly from the so-called "classic" atonement theories of later centuries. While the initial move towards the intellectualization of ideas about the relationship between Jesus and the need to account for sinfulness can be seen in the letter to the Hebrews (see Chapter Five, for instance), these later theories unashamedly begin from the intellectual problem of sin and seek to provide a theological remedy that is inevitably articulated in the language and context of a particular time.

Today we live in an age in which we understand the world in terms of replaceable theories and evolving models of knowledge. We prioritize embodied experience over notions of once-for-all revelation. Do we really expect people to give much, if any, credence to Anselm's eleventh century "juridical theory" that sees Jesus' death as settling the unpaid debt of God's affronted honor? And in the light of our reading of Jeremiah, where God supersedes the Abrahamic covenant of blood in favor of one of mutuality, can we really promote the idea (found originally in Hebrews) that, *as an act of love,* God willingly assented to sacrifice Jesus by putting him to death in our place? Can we really see merit or logic in the belief that the death of a person in the past can either atone for acts committed by people today or in the future or for an act committed by mythical figures in a garden-paradise past? Can that past understanding of atonement ever bring peace of mind or be the foundation for mature faith for anyone except someone whose normal life or perspective is that of a victim, a scapegoat, or a casualty of radical injustice? And if we imagine that Jesus is being perpetually crucified somewhere for our ongoing sinfulness, then what sort of God does that leave us with? What sort of God actually requires punitive appeasement, except just another "god-among-other-gods"? The God of punitive appeasement is certainly not the God whom Jeremiah came to know. Moreover, if an understanding of creation as an open-ended, unfolding process flowing from the dynamic nature of God is one that makes sense, and if we know there was no historical Adam and Eve and that the idea of original sin serves as a metaphor for an awareness of our inherent imperfection, *there can be no Great Fall, no One-Event-In-The-Past for which any atonement is required.*

Atonement is, then, either an idea to be discarded as functionally meaningless or one to be reconstructed for our own times. Atonement becomes a way of *articulating our experience* of a newly recreated relationship with God, with Jesus, with self, and with neighbor. In other words, atonement becomes "*at-one-ment.*" Atonement becomes a means to articulate the experience of the ever-unfolding process of receiving the grace of new insights about ourselves and God. Atonement leads to recommitting ourselves to beginning again and, indeed, to going further on the journey with Jesus, experienced in our flesh as "Lord and savior."

Resurrection

If creation is an ongoing process, then atonement is none other than the mechanism by which we experience and participate in God's re-creative being. By becoming channels of re-creation for others, resurrection is not just a singular event in Gethsemane or something that happens only after our death, but the sign and seal of the promise that God has walked away from blood covenants and the desire for sacrifice. The resurrection—re-creation in God—is an ongoing reality witnessed and experienced at all times and forever in the person of Jesus.

This understanding of resurrection demonstrates that the traditional atonement theories—whereby a mandatory confession of guilt necessarily precedes and is a requirement for the experience of forgiveness—is contrary to the mechanism of God's creative activity and nature. God does not require that we make an intellectual statement of guilt before we can be forgiven; rather God freely gives us the experience of re-creative and venturesome love and grace to which we are then free to respond by confession.

And this is so because God is not just "a god-among-other-gods," a god who demands intimidation and vengeance before clemency is granted, a god who needs to exercise power over creation before mercy can be shown. To insist that we must confess guilt before we can experience forgiveness suggests that faith is merely an intellectual assertion made without making any tangible difference in how we live. To insist that we must confess our need of a remedy for sinfulness, which is based entirely on the myth of a mistake made by two people who never existed, is to condemn ourselves to live on the inside of a vicious circle that can only spiral down to death. To insist that we must confess our belief in theories of atonement that belie our experience of living, where we learn from our mistakes (or not) in an ongoing process of being recreated, is to generate a climate in which our imperfections and failings are allowed to develop into unjustifiable levels of neurotic guilt requiring constant confession or else fester into life-sapping and appalling shame that must remain forever unresolved and toxic.

This understanding of atonement is a misguided attempt to assuage anxiety and pain and can only result in producing people who are obliged to bolster their sense of well-being by locating themselves *over against* those who are identified as "outside the fold." This understanding of atonement leads people to nourish self worth by "feeding" on those who are "unforgiven," "unacceptable," and "unsaved." Such people, by needing to feel they belong within the body of "the saved," are inevitably implicated in the perpetuation of a closed system of thought and action that fails to offer anyone a way into flourishing and newness of life.

What the resurrection surely demonstrates is that atonement occurs when we experience God's re-creative love, manifest supremely at that moment of collapse we call crucifixion. Atonement brings us *to the inside of God's unconditional regenerative loving*. And the resurrection demonstrates that atonement occurs when we dare to follow the example of Jesus by following a hunch, consenting to an intuition, staking our lives on the biblical witness that God is more than "a god-among-other-gods," ultimately, that God does not deal in death. Atonement occurs whenever we experience God's invitation to participate in the journey into newness and flourishing and to explore together the "yet-more" of God and of humanity. This is the vocation of the church.

Hope for the church

But like the Israelites in Jeremiah's day, the church is in exile, in a lost, nowhere sort of place. Like the Israelites of Moses' day, the church is wandering in circles in a wilderness, alienated from itself and from the experience that called it into life. Has God given up on the church?

Exile is possibly the very place where God has called the church to be: in a desert where all kinds of things can suddenly burst into life and flourish and out of which all sorts of unexpected good things might come. Perhaps the church might be seen as living in an alien city full of unfamiliar customs and practices, full of strange people speaking a new and unintelligible language, a city that nevertheless holds within it the obscure, still-veiled hint of a promise of new beginnings and of a "yet-more" to be discovered.

This hidden "yet-more" is a consistent theme in Scripture, and it witnesses to the dynamic nature of God. God's characteristic action is to use the relationship with humanity as a means to invite us to explore and interact with God, thereby revealing what is hidden. Just like the fire that burns without being confined within predictable and logical behaviors, God is hidden within the texts of Scripture without being confined or reduced to any interpretive act of our own devising. God's hiddenness is an invitation to us to explore and journey together. And while we may never arrive at the other side of what is hidden, it may, nevertheless, be granted us to enter the darkness and encounter something that might change us forever.

Time to think about your own experience

In a time of silence you may now wish to consider your answers to the following questions. If you are with others in a group you may choose to share your responses with them.

- The film *The Matrix* describes a world where humanity was deluded into thinking that society is wonderful and flourishing—a lie that is perpetuated by those in power. Is such a scenario really possible and, if so, how might it apply to the church?

- Where do you think your ultimate security lies? How important is it to believe unerringly what you were once taught? Do you feel that openness to what is new, novel, and still uncertain is as good a way of finding "fullness of life"?

- How do you understand authority? Something that comes from Scripture and the church's tradition or something that has to be earned and given by people? Which is more important? Are there alternative understandings of authority?

- How do you explain what atonement means and what it says about the nature of God? What do you feel about the idea that your experience of the risen Jesus and the resurrection life is sufficient atonement for you before God?

Second Isaiah:
The Treasures of the Darkness

God's hidden presence is a perennial theme explored by the human authors of the Bible. The presence of God fills the pages of the Bible; the multi-layered texts of Scripture both disclose God's presence and also conceal it. Often God's hiddenness is expressed in terms of "being veiled;" for example, God is covered by a cloud on Sinai (Ex 24:16). In another text, God places Moses in a cleft in the rock and shields him with a hand (33:20–23); God's glory, the enormity of the divine presence and reality, requires the protection or the veiling of the human psyche, whose integrity would be shattered by exposure to the immensity of God's self-revelation.

Sometimes the idea of God's hiddenness emphasizes the essential unknowability of God, whose ways are not our ways (Isa 55:8). Sometimes it is the language of "darkness" that stands as a metaphor for the hidden "yet-more" of God's being and character. Traditionally God is thought to exist beyond or outside darkness (literally, above it and distinct from it); God created the earth, the earth was a "formless void" (Gen 1:2), and there was darkness. Darkness remained the original state of things until God separated light out of darkness to create day (1:3).

Darkness as gift

Despite its divine origin, centuries of dualistic thinking have turned darkness into the negative opposite of all we associate with light and goodness. Consequently, darkness almost always appears in Scripture as a negative concept or as a metaphor for uncharted danger and risk. Although Scripture often uses the idea of light to describe the presence and action of God in the world, darkness frequently represents the absence of (the gaze of) God or God's disapproval and anger. Very few biblical writers imagined God's immanence within darkness. The most notable exception is the possibly blind author of Psalm 139 who realized that God has no preference for light or dark (Hull 133). In this psalm, God dwells equally in darkness as in light:

> If I say, "Surely the darkness shall cover me,
>   and the light around me become night,"
> even the darkness is not dark to you;
>   the night is as bright as the day,
>   for darkness is as light to you. (Ps 139:11–12)

God's immanence in the darkness cannot be enlightened by the human mind or unaided reason; it requires revelation by God. Darkness, therefore, represents God's radically unknowable but creative and dynamic nature, a nature that remains forever beyond our capacity to imagine and articulate.

God's essential hiddenness and darkness stand as a precondition for intimacy with God; hiddenness and darkness are the very ground for meeting with God and symbolic of the fundamental uncertainty about the outcome of such a risk-filled encounter. As we approach God, as we enter the terrifying darkness of God's primal unknowability, we experience the inadequacy of language. We cannot use language to reduce or tame God into an object of human understanding. In an encounter in darkness the questions we might bring all fail and fall away.

What results from this ambivalent and uncertain engagement

is a wordless and imageless intimacy, a new way of experiencing God, akin perhaps to the connection between a newborn infant and its mother. We experience a way of getting on the inside of God's relationship with humanity thereby releasing new potential and new life. Darkness serves as an invitation for us to reach out, explore (if we dare) and be touched by God in unexpected and life-changing ways.

The dichotomy between the veil that hides God and protects humanity and the darkness in which God invites human encounter is also evident in the many references to God's "face." The biblical narratives reflect this ambivalence. On the one hand, the texts sometimes suggest that we are prevented from seeing the face of God by the limitations of our mortality: "no one shall see me and live" (Ex 33:20). On the other hand, Jacob sees God's face and his "life is preserved" (Gen 32:30), and Moses saw God "face to face, as one speaks to a friend" (Ex 33:11). God's face is a symbol of God's essential presence, and God's face may be "turned from humanity" and hidden: "O LORD ... Why do you hide your face from me?" (Ps 88:14) or else turned toward us and revealed:

> The LORD bless you and keep you;
> the LORD make his face shine upon you ...
> the LORD lift up his countenance upon you ...
>   (Num 6:24–26)

God's hiddenness and the future

While being held by the divine gaze always brings a blessing and results in creativity and newness, God's self is fundamentally hidden or "in darkness"—"Truly, you are a God who hides himself" (Isa 45:15). Several passages suggest that what God conceals in darkness, pending disclosure and discovery, is symbolic of the "yet-more" of God's future revelation; the darkness holds out the promise of the novelty and newness that God is preparing to birth at any moment. In these scriptural references darkness is not presented as a negative thing nor is hiddenness a metaphor for evil, danger, or chaos. Rather, the darkness is understood to contain hidden treasure—the undreamt of riches of God—and it serves to invite the extraordinary discovery, the formative revelation, that God is not "a god like other gods."

One example of this discovery occurs when Jeremiah languishes in prison after his encounters with Hananiah: "Thus says the LORD ... Call to me and I will answer you, and will tell you great and hidden things that you have not known" (Jer 33:2–3). Here the "great and hidden things" refers to the knowledge of future blessings to come upon Israel. Jeremiah is reminded that just as God created the gratuitous bounty of the earth, so will God bring about the outrageous promise of re-creation and the restoration of the people to Jerusalem.

Two further passages in Isaiah illustrate darkness as the place of hidden treasure. In the first text, God speaks to Cyrus, the "anointed," meaning the Messiah, chosen although a foreigner. Cyrus will bring about restoration. In an astonishingly powerful passage God promises to Cyrus:

> I will give you *the treasures of darkness*
> > and riches hidden in secret places ....
> I am the LORD, and there is no other ....
> I form the light and create darkness,
> > I make weal and create woe ....
> > > (Isa 45:3, 5, 7, emphasis mine)

The treasures of God's wisdom are hidden from human sight and understanding in the secret places where God's presence abides. God is waiting to turn the searing, divine gaze on those who would venture into the darkness and mystery, and this venture is dangerous and risky in the extreme. Yet God offers unimaginable and precious things to the foreign ruler Cyrus if he will enter this darkness and so be the means of delivery for God's people.

In the other passage from Isaiah, God addresses the whole nation of Israel, reminding them that they have forgotten the words spoken in the past and promises that there will be a rich, new revelation that anticipates their future homecoming:

> From this time forward I make you hear new things,
>   hidden things that you have not known.
> They are created now, not long ago;
>   before today you have never heard of them,
>   so that you could not say, "I already knew them."
> You have never heard, you have never known,
>   from of old your ear has not been opened. (Isa 48:6–8).

God promises not only to reveal things hitherto hidden, things they could not have learned even in Babylon, but God promises that these things will be utterly new, created even as the words fly from the mouth of God, things of an entirely new order and class. God promises a newness that can only be discovered by stepping into a place of adventure, a place that requires a daring openness to the "yet-more" of God. This newness can only be glimpsed through imaginative and creative human discernment. This newness comes out of what is hidden and yet is still uncreated in the deep darkness. Newness from nothing, like the flowers that blossom from the barren desert sands. Newness, freshness, ongoing generativity and flourishing that speak the very nature and character of God. New life that God brings into existence in response to the needs of God's people.

The entire book of Isaiah, but in particular "Second" Isaiah (Chapters 40–55) from where these last verses come, contains a remarkable series of meditations on the nature of God and God's interaction with the world. Second Isaiah is rooted in the Israelites' experience of their Babylonian exile, which cannot be fully appreciated without Jeremiah's description of the failure of the temple establishment, his prophecy of the Israelites' life in exile, and his account of the destruction of the whole geography of faith that reduced the Israelites to utter despair and forsakenness.

Surrender to a new blessing

Moreover, the promises and the vision for restoration articulated in Second Isaiah became a reality only for those who experienced the loss of everything. There had to be loss, grief, suffering, and abandonment before hope could be seen, felt, and articulated. There had to be a complete relinquishment and exile (explored powerfully in Jeremiah, Ezekiel, the Book of Lamentations, and Psalm 137) before Isaiah's words of hope, restoration, and liberation could have any meaningful resonance.

The Israelites' actual experience of life in Babylon was not, of course, uniformly negative. They lived in exile for several generations, marrying, prospering, raising families, and contributing to the community. Indeed, when they eventually returned to Judah, they brought back valuable new perspectives and ideas. Yet the marvelous poetry in Second Isaiah is meant to challenge these assimilating Israelites' uncritical and easy acceptance of their new circumstances and to awaken them to their exile and its impact on their inheritance. Second Isaiah speaks to the Israelites of the new but hidden things that God is creating and of the storehouses of unimaginable treasure that await them, *if they leave the security of the familiar and cross over the border into the outside and the unknown.*

Second Isaiah invites the people to face the terrifying but

inescapable ordeal of the journey homewards. They are reminded
that it is only by committing themselves to the journey out of exile,
by daring themselves to follow the call and enter the unknown
desert that separates them from their real home, that God can be
encountered and God's regenerative call heard and explored:

> A voice cries out:
> "In the wilderness prepare the way of the LORD ....
> Then the glory of the LORD shall be revealed." (Isa 40:3, 5)

> I will open rivers on the bare heights,
>   and fountains in the midst of the valleys;
> I will make the wilderness a pool of water,
>   and the dry land springs of water. (41:18)

> Sing to the LORD a new song. (42:10)

> Sing, O heavens, for the LORD has done it;
>   Shout, O depths of the earth;
> break forth into singing, O mountains,
>   O forest, and every tree in it! (44:23)

> For the LORD will comfort Zion;
>   he will comfort all her waste places,
>   and will make her wilderness like Eden,
>   her desert like the garden of the LORD. (51:3)

> Ho, everyone who thirsts, come to the waters;
> and you that have no money, come, buy and eat!
> Come, buy wine and milk without money and without
>   price. (55:1–2)

For you shall go out in joy,
    and be led back in peace;
the mountains and the hills before you
    shall burst into song,
and all the trees of the field shall clap their hands.
Instead of thorn shall come up the cypress;
    instead of the brier shall come up the myrtle;
        (55:12–13)

For God is the only source of new life. And the following verses testify that God is about to act and perform something utterly unexpected:

Do not remember the former things,
    or consider the things of old.
I am about to do a new thing;
    now it springs forth, do you not perceive it?
I will make a way in the wilderness
    and rivers in the desert. (43:18–19)

Isaiah's prophecies remind us that we cannot access God's promises of newness while we still cling to old ways: room for newness is made only by letting go of what is done and gone. Old systems that constrain God's re-creative energy and established conventions and practices that are destructive, exploitative, and resistant to truth and justice must all be examined. For God will not begin birthing newness from what currently exists; it is God's wish that we learn "a new song."

Second Isaiah reflects on darkness and newness more keenly than almost any other biblical writer. The author declares the good news that it is God's desire to bring forth "the hidden treasures of the darkness" and proclaims newness and restoration for the

Israelites. To enable the Israelites to embrace the memories of their past and understand themselves as exiles, at odds with their current condition, Isaiah reworks their historical memory. By reworking their memories, Isaiah generates a desire to engage with, enter, and explore the hiddenness, darkness, and mystery of God. Isaiah encourages the people to risk the empty wilderness so that undreamt new possibilities will be disclosed.

Israel: the suffering servant

Perhaps the most famous response to the call to enter the darkness of unknowing is that of the extraordinary figure, the so-called "suffering servant" found in Isaiah 52:13–53:12. These verses describe a figure who appears to be a beaten, bruised and dislocated victim and is a metaphor of the trauma Israel has experienced in exile and at the hands of those who would "cut [Israel] off from the land of the living" (53:8). The servant, symbolic of the people of Israel, is mocked by all who see him:

> Just as there were many who were astonished at him
>   —so marred was his appearance, beyond human
>   semblance,
>   and his form beyond that of mortals—
> so he shall startle many nations;
>   kings shall shut their mouths because of him;
> for that which had not been told them they shall see,
>   and that which they had not heard they shall
>   contemplate.
> Who has believed what we have heard?
>   And to whom has the arm of the LORD been
>   revealed?
> For he grew up before him like a young plant,
>   and like a root out of dry ground;

he had no form or majesty that we should look at him,
  nothing in his appearance that we should desire him.
He was despised and rejected by others;
  a man of suffering and acquainted with infirmity;
and as one from whom others hide their faces [or "as one
who hides his face from us"]
he was despised, and we held him of no account.
    (52:14—53:3)

The text describes how foreign kings are astonished by the
man's changed appearance. They hide their faces from him as he
hides his from them: they cannot look at each other, so badly
deformed is his figure, so great his pain. It is Israel who is despised,
rejected, and ignored by the other nations; Israel is both a victim
of their violence and a pitiable but inevitable scapegoat doomed to
death in the wilderness:

Surely he had borne our infirmities and carried our
diseases. (53:4)

He was wounded for our transgressions,
  crushed for our iniquities,
upon him was the punishment that made us whole. (53:5)

Israel is also like a lamb marked for sacrifice and unable to be
redeemed:

He was oppressed, and he was afflicted,
  yet he did not open his mouth;
like a lamb that is led to the slaughter,
and like a sheep that before its shearers is silent,
  so he did not open his mouth. (53:7)
These verses seem to state that there is no hope for Israel. And

so the nations conclude that God has clearly determined Israel's fate.

And yet the nations discover themselves to be victims of their own ignorance. For what they see as worthless and irredeemable is, in fact, God's chosen vehicle of deliverance. They are reduced to silence: utterly surprised and startled—undone by God. They knew so little of God that they were unable to be open to God's endless creativity and inventive possibility; the nations were unable to imagine the form that God's creativity might take. The nations can only stand by and watch as God unfolds a radically unanticipated alternative future for Israel:

> See, my servant shall prosper;
>> he shall be exalted and lifted up,
>> and shall be very high. (52:13)

> He shall see his offspring, and shall prolong his days;
> through him the will of the LORD shall prosper.
>> Out of his anguish he shall see light. (53:10–11)

> Therefore I will allot him a portion with the great,
>> and he shall divide the spoil with the strong;
> because he poured out himself to death,
>> and was numbered with the transgressors;
> yet he bore the sin of many,
>> and made intercession for the transgressors. (53:12)

Here is a new song: the celebration of new possibilities for Israel, the discovery of new treasures in the dark, in the hidden and awful mystery of God. Concealed beneath the bruised and tortured exterior is the face of one who consented to walk with God into the unspeakable perils of the wilderness. Here is the face of one who trusted God by complete relinquishment and exile, who has come to know God, and who has thereby come to fulfill his God-given vocation to be the servant of all the nations. God's proffered newness demands that someone risk entering the darkness in order to take the first precarious steps of trust deep into the mystery of God. And these steps are taken in the belief that God is both willing and able to create newness out of nothing, new life out of anxiety, sickness, and death.

Exploring the mystery of God, exploring how God is hidden-and-yet-revealed in the darkness, in the hiddenness of each lived moment, is one way of discovering how "fullness of life" is lived. Fullness of life is found on "the knife-edge," on the dangerous growing edge between what is and what (though about to be disclosed) still remains hidden.

Exploring the hiddenness of each moment is a way to discover how a life lived in openness to the "yet-more" of God is necessarily one lived in the dislocated space of "alert detachment." This detachment means choosing to enter the darkness of unknowing and engage with the riskiness of uncertainty and possible failure, while remaining ready to act and respond at any moment to what is both disclosed and demanded.

The song of the suffering servant of Isaiah is only one reading depicting this mode of life. Other texts describe how God's creative energy is ever at work transforming any situation, any disaster, any dark night, into an occasion for God's unexpected creativity. God's hidden nature and irrepressible desire for venturesome, creative mutuality and connectedness with humanity is ever ready to be revealed.

Time to think about your own experience

In a time of silence you may now wish to consider your answers to the following questions. If you are with others in a group you may choose to share your responses with them.

- Have you ever felt that God is hiding something from you? What would you like God to reveal? Have you ever looked into a mirror at your face, or at the faces of others, and considered what is revealed there about God? How would you like God to look at you?

- How do you understand those portions of the Book of Isaiah that describe the so-called "suffering servant"? What is your experience of finding God or meaning in suffering? Can suffering ever be good for you?

- Have you ever experienced God calling you out of your "comfort zone" into a place that you find unpleasant, challenging, or scary? What may God be challenging you to reconsider in the light of what Isaiah had to say to the exiles about finding God through risk and danger?

- How do you know if you are sufficiently open to the "yet-more" about God and to being surprised by God? What new things would you like God to offer you? What new song do you need to learn?

CHAPTER 5-B

Toward a Theology that Re-imagines the World: On Darkness, Birth, and Flourishing

For Christians the suffering figure found in Isaiah is generally interpreted to be the crucified Jesus. Indeed this interpretation is so dominant that many Christians may find it difficult to engage with these texts differently or to read them in any other way. In fact, in order to read these texts in a new way, what is needed is a considerable willingness to "unlearn," to remember that Isaiah has been interpreted differently over time, and to recognize that God is hidden from us in the multi-layered complexity of Scripture. God always is more than the sum of any single reading or any hermeneutical tradition.

Isaiah and the passion narratives

Isaiah's suffering servant had a fundamental impact on the portrayal of the passion and death of Jesus in the Gospels. This impact is due in part because the earliest evangelist, Mark, chose Isaiah as the interpretive framework for understanding the ministry of Jesus (Mk 1:2–3) and because Jesus apparently identified his mission (Lk 4:16–19) with the implementation of God's reign as expressed in Isaiah (Isa 61:1–2, 58:6). For the evangelist the use of Isaiah, along with certain references from the Psalms, created a prophetic link between Isaiah's suffering and redemptive figure and the meaning of Jesus' death. This link allowed Christians to see that God's act of radical newness was located in Jesus rather than in the Israelite nation. Yet both Jesus as the suffering servant and the nation of Israel as the suffering servant must surely be allowed to stand; God clearly honors both.

While there are minimal direct textual references in the passion narratives to the suffering servant texts in Isaiah, because of the deep associations cultivated throughout the history of the Christian tradition and their continuous liturgical use, the suffering servant texts add the nuances of feeling and insight that are not found in the Gospel accounts of the passion. Indeed, Jesus' physical appearance and emotions during his passion and crucifixion are barely depicted in the Gospels. The Gospels confine themselves almost entirely to the narrative action and to those

details that identify and locate Jesus within a framework of
meaning that seeks to make sense of his death.

Darkness and the crucifixion

In the Gospel accounts of Jesus' crucifixion, the themes of
darkness, abandonment, and the hiddenness and unknowability
of God all resurface. Jesus is mocked, scorned, and marked for
death. He is recognized as one who (like the suffering figure of
Isaiah) was born to rejection and was forsaken, apparently even
by God. For Jesus, the crucifixion was the very unraveling of the
certainty and trust in God as his father that Jesus had discovered
at his baptism. The cross stands in stark contrast to the sudden
experience of light, by which the early church symbolized the full
significance of Jesus' ministry for the Jewish temple: "And the
curtain of the temple was torn in two, from top to bottom"
(Mk 15:38).

Inner darkness overwhelmed Jesus with feelings that God had
turned away and was hidden from him, and physical darkness
covered the land. The reference in Mark to darkness at midday:
"When it was noon, darkness came over the whole land until three
in the afternoon" (15:33) is complemented by Jesus' cry of
dereliction and abandonment: "At three o'clock Jesus cried out
with a loud voice, '*Eloi, Eloi, lema sabachthani?*' which means, 'My
God, my God, why have you forsaken me?'" (15:34).

And yet Jesus' cry, "My God, my God ..." shows how, even at
the point of death and recognition of the apparent failure of his
mission, *Jesus will not let God go.* He will not let God forget the
mutuality, the covenant, established between them that day in the
Jordan. For at his baptism, Jesus consented to follow his intuition
that he had to walk a particular path and pursue it faithfully to the
end whatever the outcome. He said "Yes!" to God and trusted in
the father-and-son relationship he had discerned. Jesus opted to

rely on this relationship, even in the darkest of moments, even during those trials that would surely come and whose sufferings, demands, and ultimate outcome he could never know or begin to imagine. Jesus dared believe that God would be with him in the darkness and on the other side of catastrophe. Jesus' so-called "cry of dereliction" reveals that God was real for Jesus. Even in the darkness, even when Jesus couldn't grasp or feel the divine presence, God was there: hidden but abiding, unknowable but strangely dependable. Jesus trusted that God was all the while working to bring re-creation out of chaos.

From the hidden heart of the darkness, from the anguish of utter collapse and annihilation, God produces newness and unimaginable new life. With Jesus, God's creativity takes a new form: resurrection. From within the darkness of an empty tomb God utters Easter, and the world is forever changed; the world is completely re-imagined in the face of God's extraordinary creativity.

If Jesus' experience teaches anything, it is that we need to reflect on our experiences of darkness and alienation. We need to reflect on our feelings of powerlessness, disillusionment, and abandonment. We need to reflect especially on the vague memories of a certain "something more" that eludes us: the desire for connection that we are so desperate to recapture.

Theological imagination

One prophetic task to which the church is called is to enable people to create spaces to reflect imaginatively on the "as-yet-still-hidden," on those obscure and unarticulated alternatives to current perceptions of existence and meaning. Our task as Christians is to learn to reflect imaginatively on the "yet-more" of God. And this reflection process needs to include the practice and development of theological and poetic imagination, which is the most subversive and liberating act that a faith community can undertake. To practice and develop theological and poetic imagination, we must be prepared, like Jesus, to enter into the darkness and the unknown that enfolds our human limitations. We must walk the path that leads us beyond what is safe and comfortable to the risky hidden places where God abides and where we are called to encounter God afresh.

We need to consider how multi-layered metaphors such as Isaiah's "treasures of darkness and riches hidden in secret places," and Jesus' cry howled into the darkness, "My God, my God, why … ?" might lead us to the "yet-more" that God proffers to each of us. This task is an urgent and demanding call to discernment. For God's newness comes, not only in the form of radical renewal, but also as the unexpected and unimaginable in discontinuous novelty, unrelated to anything that has come before. There are unrecognizable things that God may even now be creating for us. God's hidden treasure house is ever overflowing with possibilities.

Discerning God in the darkness

But what does it mean today to talk of God "abiding hidden in darkness" or of God "turning away from us?" We may no longer share the anthropomorphic perspective of Scripture (where God literally has a face and really hides in the darkness); instead we understand that all language about God is metaphorical. We use language to create images about God; we know the value of prose and poetry, we understand about rhetorical devices, simile, and metaphor. We know that, however much we try, language cannot capture the meaning of anything; for while a word may more or less carry the weight of what it is meant to signify, in fact its entire meaning forever eludes our grasp. And if the reality of something ordinary is always greater than the language and images used to describe it, how much more will God evade our intellect?

When we talk of God, famously described by Anselm of Canterbury as that "than which nothing greater can be conceived," (Anselm 2.1) we are aware of the limitations of language. Words and images will take us only so far. And while we may travel a little further if we allow ourselves to use the multivalency of poetry, due to the "extra space for meaning" that poetry allows through its use of juxtaposition, contraposition, alliteration and so on, eventually words are never enough; we soon come to the end of them and to silence. The fullness of God is ultimately both unknowable and unspeakable.

From our human perspective God is, to a greater or lesser extent, always hidden inside or even hidden on the far side of language. Language is actually a veil of darkness drawn over the face of God, hiding the essence of God behind the many verbs, adverbs, and adjectives describing God's action in the world. Language can reveal so much, but it then must inevitably be set aside. Likewise, we can enter so far in prayer and meditation using images and language, and then we can go no further.

When we arrive at the limits of knowledge, it may (or may not) be granted us to enter and explore the silent darkness where God is encountered and so find ourselves transformed by God. And if we are permitted to enter, we may perhaps return to the world knowing we have "been somewhere," but we may be unable to say much, if anything, to describe our experience other than the vague memory, the suggestion, that God has drawn close and touched us.

Apophatic spirituality

This primary unknowability of God is often termed apophatic or "negative" spirituality, a prayer discipline that sets aside thoughts, concepts, and emotions when trying to experience God.

This form of prayer seeks to peel away—to unlearn—the traditional attributes, titles, and descriptions of God in order to arrive at a place "beyond" where God may be disclosed as God truly is. This approach is characteristic of the theology of the Eastern or Orthodox Church from as early as the third century. Clement of Alexandria (200 CE) described the act of drawing near to God as approaching an abyss:

> If, then, ... we cast ourselves into the greatness of Christ, and thence advance into immensity by holiness, we may reach somehow to the conception of the Almighty, knowing not what He is, but what He is not. (Clement 5:11)

The more we travel on our journey with God, the more we will have a kind of knowledge of God that is intuitive rather than rational. The more we "advance," the more we will have to surrender or to deny what we previously believed we understood about God with our thinking mind. The more we let go, the more we have to risk—even to the point of entering into the terrible abyss itself, that "secret place" beyond rational thought and language where the "treasures of the darkness" may be found.

Another early theologian Gregory of Nyssa (died, 395 CE) echoes Clement: "One does not know God except in terms of our incapacity to apprehend him" (Leech 1:143). And by the end of the fifth century, the influential theologian Dionysius the Areopagite was able to speak of a *theology of silence*, of a place beyond the understanding accessed only by a process of unlearning (Dionysius 5). This unlearning was a painful stripping away both of the layers of personal identity and of the intellectual apparatus (language, ideas, and feelings) by which people claim to understand God.

The apophatic or negative theological language was never

common in the Western church that was, from early in the second millennium at least, dominated by a widespread devotion to the apostolic life and to following the example of the earthly Jesus in daily life. Yet by the fourteenth century in Northern Europe, it is possible to identify the presence of two different approaches to negative theology or to the *via negativa*, as it was known.

Theologians like Eckhart (died, c.1328) and John Tauler (died, 1361) held that, in order to draw near to God, a person had to transcend all language and images and relinquish all that was superfluous and superficial. This involved the yielding of those senses, actions, and practices that might have hitherto supported devotion or worship, as well as the surrendering of the normal faculties of knowing or cognition. The purpose of this abandonment was to become known by "the only One who knows" and to be united with God on an intuitive or "intellective" level.

In contrast writers like John Ruusbroec (died, 1381) and the unknown author of the *Cloud of Unknowing* (written in England in the late fourteenth century) attempted to describe their experience of God. These writers held that, rather than coming to knowledge of God on an intellectual level, a person entered into a union with God solely through love, like the act of union between two lovers, a spontaneous, all-consuming self-giving.

Into the divine darkness

Both approaches, however, hold that drawing near to God requires an entry into a kind of divine darkness and runs the risk of being plunged into an abyssal nothingness, a place where God's hiddenness is unveiled, a place of profound and direct experience of God. Here we must painfully abandon our rationality, our facility for objective knowing and conceptualizing, and in exchange receive an awareness of being a creature made in the likeness of God, an awareness of being known and loved by God, and of sharing in a relationship that is mutual, creative, and loving. Eckhart writes:

> God is foolishly in love with us, it seems he has forgotten heaven and earth and … his entire business seems with me alone, to give me everything to comfort me; he gives it to me suddenly, he gives it to me wholly, he gives it to me perfect, he gives it all the time and he gives it to all creatures. (Pfeiffer 231)

At such moments we become aware that what is revealed of God's nature is God's essential generativity and that ceaseless creativity whose "ultimate purpose is birth" (227). In language that anticipates Hannah Arendt, Eckhart continues:

> It belongs to all creatures to be born. A creature without birth would not be at all. … It is a sign of the divine birth that all creatures are wrought in it. (199)

> Birth is always happening. (3)

> The Father never stops (150)

Eckhart describes how, in the power of the Spirit, God's creative energy blossoms and flowers and brings forth love: "In this power is God, ever verdant, flowering in all the joy and glory of his actual self" (36) and "the flower that blossoms, love, is the Holy Ghost." (154)

To be caught up in the darkness of God, on the other side of the intellectual annihilation and the painful physical disorientation of senses and identity, is to discover that God never ceases to create and bring forth newness and resurrection. God's entire concern is with the birthing of the Son into the world and the human soul:

> God is looking at the soul and the soul is looking at God.
> ... [and God desires that] we there abide in utter
> destitution and so enable God at all times without ceasing
> to bring his one-begotten Son to birth .... This birth
> befalls not once a year nor once a day nor once an hour,
> but all the time. (117)

The birthing of the Son stands as a metaphor for God's ceaseless regenerative activity visible in the ongoing process of creation and resurrection at work in the human soul:

> God is ever at work in the eternal now, and his work is the
> begetting of his Son; he is bringing him forth all the while.
> In his birth all things have proceeded forth, and so great is
> his pleasure in this birth that he spends his whole energy
> upon it. ... God makes all creatures in a word, but in order
> to vivify the soul the whole of his power is expended in his
> Son .... In his birth [the soul] comes to life .... God speaks
> himself in his Son. (199)

Moreover, God brings new life and radical newness into the world when and wherever new acts of justice happen:

> At every virtue of the just God is born and is rejoiced ...
> every act done by the just, is nothing but the Son being
> begotten by the Father. ... [God] is always trying to beget
> his Son. (149, 150)

This view of God is theologically and spiritually very attractive because it recognizes humanity as both part of creation and yet

called to be something different, something more. This view
suggests that, like Jesus, we are called to explore and respond to
what it means to bring forth the spark of the divine that is within
each one of us. It also acknowledges that creation by God, salvation
through Christ, and social justice are intrinsically interwoven. For
the task of the embodied soul is to be transfigured through acts of
prophetic justice and thereby help transform the world.

Johannes Tauler portrays the union with God, the spark or
moment of God's birthing of the Son, as an event in the dark
hidden heart of a person's most authentic self. And Tauler often
uses the metaphor "the *ground* of the soul" for this most hidden of
places (where God, not the senses or the intellect) is active:

> Some receive the Holy Spirit by way of their senses ...
> Others receive Him in a loftier manner, by way of their
> higher powers ... The third group receives Him beyond
> mode or manner, within that hidden abyss, that secret
> realm, that blissful ground ... No created light can touch
> this ground and illuminate it, for it is truly God's home
> and dwelling-place. (Tauler 80, 147)

Tauler's use of the word *ground* suggests that God meets us at our
most fundamental level, in the bedrock of our being, the soul. The
use of ground also suggests the idea of the soil, the hidden darkness
in which things germinate and spring forth and which needs careful
preparation in order to bear fruit. Once prepared by God and infused
by the Spirit, however, this darkness of the soul is the source of
extravagant new growth, which flourishes and blossoms:

> In all this we should proceed precisely like a farmer ....
> [and] work deeply into our ground, examine it, and turn it
> over thoroughly. ... As soon as the outer man has

prepared his lower and higher faculties, the whole of him
becomes receptive, and the tender, divine sun begins to
send its rays into his noble ground; and now a joyous
summer commences, a downright may-blossoming is about
to unfold. The gracious, eternal God permits the spirit to
green and bloom and bring forth the most marvelous fruit.
(85–86)

A greening God

This language of flourishing and blossoming, of verdancy and
greening, has its roots in the darkness of prayer experienced by
that extraordinary group of women mystics known collectively as
the Beguines. The Beguines, who flourished in the Low Countries
from the twelfth to the early sixteenth century, spoke from a
unique experience of the spiritual life because of their gender. And
they used language, images, and metaphors that were problematic
for the ecclesiastical authorities. Many of Tauler's sermons were
preached for these spiritual women; both he and Eckhart
influenced the thought of those among whom they ministered and
preached; in turn, these men were influenced by the alternative
imagination of the women.

The Beguine Hadewijch of Brabant (thirteenth century), for
example, likens God's love to cooling dew and moistness, a flowing
spring and the flourishing water of life:

> Living spring, her sixth name,
> Is truly appropriate to Love after that of dew.
> This flowing forth and this reflux
> Of one into the other, and this growth in God,
> Surpass the mind and understanding,
> The intelligence and capacity
> Of human creatures.

But still we have it in our nature:
The hidden ways where Love makes us walk
And where she lets us receive, amid blows, that sweet kiss—
Here it is that we receive that sweet living life,
So that Life shall give life in our life. (Hadewijch 356)

Hadewijch describes how, in the darkness beyond the human intellectual realm, lay "the hidden ways" where love gushes forth from God into the human soul and back again into God, flowing between the two and nourishing new life and bringing flourishing. Her language, revealing the influence of contemporary courtly love poetry, is very similar to that of Beguine Mechthild of Magdeburg (died, c.1282):

How the soul speaks to God:

Lord, you are my lover,
My longing,
My flowing stream,
My sun,
And I am your reflection. (Bowie 55)

How God answers the soul:

It is my nature that makes me love you often,
For I am love itself.

It is my longing that makes me love you intensely,
For I yearn to be loved from the heart.

It is my eternity that makes me love you long,
For I have no end. (56)

The power of love:

Love penetrates the senses and storms the soul with all its power. When love grows in the soul, then it rises up with great longing to God and flowingly expands to receive the miracle that breaks in upon it. Love melts through the soul and into the senses. (71)

Similar experiences are described in the writings of the more famous Hildegard of Bingen (died, 1178), who, although not a Beguine, clearly shares the same common heritage of language and visualization:

Hail, branch most verdant ....

When the time came
for your boughs to blossom ...
the warm sun distilled in you
a perfume like balsam.

For in you bloomed the fair flower
that made all the spices fragrant,
dry though they were,
and they all burst into verdure. (Newman 193)

The striking imagery of the mutual ebb and flow of love, of growth and expansion, and of the creative relationship between God and the human soul speaks eloquently of the nature of the mystical explorations of these women. Their reflections offer a profound testimony both to the powerfully regenerative nature of their experience of the darkness and hiddenness of God and to the fresh ways these women sought to articulate their experience of the connection between God and creation. Needless to say, these women were often misunderstood by the men charged with their pastoral care. Their language and imagery suggested a direct experience of God that was unacceptable to the church authorities. The sad case of Margaret Porete is but one example among many of the censure and punishment that was meted out to them (Sheldrake 152).

These mystics, male as well as female, have much to teach us. They can help us re-imagine our world by giving us a language with which to articulate the desire for, and experience of, human flourishing. From their example of courage and daring we can learn to enter the deep darkness that holds our world in its embrace and so experience God. They can inspire us to discern our connectedness to the universe that is our home. They can help us to courageously accept the limitations and boundaries of our capacity to know and to control. And they can teach us to befriend the darkness within each of us.

Our own call to walk the outer edges of experience

Whenever we feel ourselves engulfed by a deep and impenetrable darkness, when we feel alone, alienated, and exiled in a universe that we fear is terrifyingly devoid of meaning and purpose, when we experience a gnawing paranoia that makes us want to flee the darkness, we must dare ourselves to overcome the promptings we feel within us and respond to God's call to remain in the darkness. Like Jesus and like Isaiah's suffering servant, we must dare ourselves to risk all and step into the unknown. We must remain within the dark as long as we are able to and so discover, for ourselves and for others, that the darkness is not the end, that the darkness is not the last word. For the darkness is not a barren, empty wilderness but a place that is alive, vital, and glowing with love.

The revelation that links Isaiah with Jesus and both of them with Christian mystics across the centuries is that the darkness holds, not sterile fear, but richly fecund treasure. To walk the dangerous outer edges of human knowledge, to accept the risk of losing ourselves in the nameless darkness, to experience abandonment away from the safe familiarity of home, is to accept that life must be lived in openness to the "yet-more" of God. Unless we are open to accepting and embracing pain and suffering (and all that lies hidden within it) we can never be open to recognizing and welcoming God's newness when it comes. Unless we are open to accepting and embracing the terrible darkness, we cannot celebrate the new creation, birth, and flourishing that is always God's wish for us. What Jesus shows us supremely is how to risk annihilation and let go all we hold dear (knowledge, identity, security, even life itself) and to open ourselves up to the "yet-more" of God.

As the body of Christ in the world, it is the church's God-given task to articulate a theology of darkness for a world living in alienation, desperately seeking home, and in need of the undreamt-of possibilities that the darkness contains. The gift that Jesus bequeaths us for this great task is the discovery that God will not disappoint us if we dare to say "Yes!"

Time to think about your own experience

In a time of silence you may now wish to consider your answers to the following questions. If you are with others in a group you may choose to share your responses with them.

- Do you think Jesus knew that resurrection would follow after three days or do you think that Jesus really believed God abandoned him? Is God revealed completely in Jesus? Or given the inevitable limitations of Jesus' humanity, were there things about God that Jesus did not know?

- Do you like the darkness? What does the idea represent for you or for society at large? Is all darkness black and empty? Is darkness a friendly place? What difference does the idea that God made the darkness, as well as the light, make to you? How might you begin to experience God "in the darkness"?

- How do you respond to the idea that God wishes nothing more than for the Son to be born in us? How does this idea fit with your experience? What would it mean for the church to understand its mission as birthing Jesus into the world?

- Many of the medieval female mystics experienced their relationship with God in terms of flowing water, living springs of love, and God's flourishing and nurturing of all life. How might this experience of God be good news for people today? How is it consistent with the teaching and ministry of Jesus?

Jesus, Bodies, and the Threat of Wholeness

The idea of "flourishing" occurs frequently in the Hebrew Scriptures. The verb *parach* means "to flourish, bud, blossom, sprout, shoot, bloom, break open/forth" and occurs twenty-four times in eleven different books of the Hebrew Scripture. This verb occurs most numerously in Isaiah:

> The wilderness and the dry land shall be glad,
>   the desert shall rejoice and blossom;
> like the crocus it shall blossom abundantly. (Isa 35:1–2)

And again:

> You shall see, and your heart shall rejoice;
>   your bodies shall flourish like the grass;
> and it shall be known that the hand of the LORD is with his servants,
>   and his indignation is against his enemies. (66:14)

The verb *tzutz* means "to blossom" and "to flourish." This verb occurs nine times (chiefly in the Psalms, for example, "May people blossom in the cities like the grass of the field" [Ps 72:16]). The verb *raanan*, meaning "to be green or verdant, to grow luxuriantly" and "to flourish" is found nineteen times, including both in the Psalms and Jeremiah:

> In old age they still produce fruit;
>   they are always green and full of sap. (Ps 92:14)

Blessed are those who trust in the LORD,
>   whose trust is the LORD.
They shall be like a tree planted by water,
>   sending out its roots by the stream.
It shall not fear when heat comes,
>   and its leaves shall stay green. (Jer 17:7–8)

People flourish just as the plants, fruits, or flowers do.
Flourishing is a sign that the regenerative presence of God is near,
a sign that people open themselves up to God's *shalom* (God's
healing and wholeness) and discover themselves blessed by God.
Indeed, understanding creation as ongoing unstoppable outpouring
of creativity, where God speaking is God creating, suggests that to
be created is to be blessed and that to receive a spoken blessing
from God necessarily carries with it a practical and physical *benefit*
(literally "an act of doing good"). God's blessing re-creates the
individuals and communities concerned. So to be blessed by God is
inevitably to flourish.

Flourishing becomes salvation

The New Testament hardly ever mentions "flourishing" in the
sense mentioned above. There are, however, many references to
"fullness" or "completeness" (Greek, *pleroma*) and "abundance"
(Greek, *perisseia*). Most of these references are *not* associated with
the Gospel accounts of Jesus' healing ministry, which suggests that
in the early church the relationship between flourishing and the
healing of the human body has given way to a new idea: that
fullness or abundance of life is bound up with the need for
salvation.

Of course the notion of flourishing lies behind the idea of
salvation, since both have their roots in the broad concept of
shalom or "wholeness." It is salvation, however, that dominates the

identity, theology, and proclamation of Christianity, particularly in the West. Salvation has come to mean rescue from the "temptations of the flesh and the body" and deliverance from "sin, the world, and the devil." The idea of salvation encourages a preference for the certain joys of a blissful afterlife rather than the "fleeting pleasures" of the physical here-and-now. Moreover, salvation is often expressed as an event for oneself (individual, family, congregation, church, me and us) and for those who are the same as us. Salvation is articulated "over against" other people (those outside) and those who are different.

This understanding of salvation depends on a developed notion of humanity's fall from a once-perfect state, of sin, atonement, and the need for restoration by a sacrificial act of a savior figure. And on this notion hangs the vast weight of church teaching and practice about salvation that has arguably done little to help people flourish and find the life in abundance that Jesus came to offer.

Surely the belief that God actually became incarnate in human flesh suggests that the *physical body* (and the communities of bodies that make up human society) is the site of human flourishing. The incarnation of God in Jesus allows two things to happen: God is exposed to the possibilities of life lived in the flesh and, in the newly visible divinity, humanity sees fresh options for living and discovers what it means for all human flesh (each individual human body) to be creative and to flourish after the image of God. The human body is the place where this exchange happens: God experiences life in flesh and our bodies become the place where "what-it-is-to-be-like-God" is revealed and known—at least insofar as the limitations of our physical bodies allow us to bear. And if the body is the arena in which we experience flourishing and if the incarnation is to be good news, this experience and this good news must be *for all human beings.*

The body in the Gospels

The body is a dominant theme in the Gospels: physical, gendered, diseased, and disabled. Bodies are healed (or sometimes not healed) by touch or by prayer. The New Testament presents the place and meaning of bodies in the community, the experience of life as an embodied social creature, the resurrection of bodies and, of course, the idea that the Christian community itself may be likened to a body—that of the risen and ascended Jesus. In the Gospels Jesus goes from place to place touching and healing diseased and distressed bodies; he embraces bodies ostracized from the temple and from social relationships and restores bodies back to the community. In other words, Jesus offers wholeness and flourishing to both individuals and communities, and he does so by enabling them to flourish as bodies within the body of the community. Wherever he goes he turns "no-bodies" into "some-bodies":

> They came to Bethsaida. Some people brought a blind
> man to him and begged him to touch him. He took the
> blind man by the hand and led him out of the village; and
> when he had put saliva on his eyes and laid his hands on
> him, he asked him, "Can you see anything?" And the man
> looked up and said, "I can see people, but they look like
> trees, walking." Then Jesus laid his hands on his eyes
> again; and he looked intently and his sight was restored,
> and he saw everything clearly. Then he sent him away to
> his home, saying, "Do not even go into the village." (Mk
> 8:22–26)

Here Jesus demonstrates the unconditional love and "wholeness-making" that results wherever God's newness and re-creation is at work. Time after time Jesus releases individuals from what has oppressed them in the past so they can flourish and embrace fullness of life as their physical bodies (their embodied selves) are *re-incorporated* within the body of the community.

This is hardly surprising. For Jesus came to literally embody God's "speaking-creating," that is, God's regenerative voice and re-creative action. Jesus enacts the promise of abundance of life (Jn 10:10) that is given gratuitously by God to those who seek it—word to flesh, body to body, his body to their body.

Jesus and God

But how exactly does Jesus enable this abundant life? How is he part of the process of healing and wholeness-making? What is it about him that allows God's creative energy to flow and allow people to flourish and find fullness of life? And is it possible to read and understand Jesus in a way that frees him from being the unique all-powerful savior figure and sole agent of salvation for humanity? For this is a role he seems generally unwilling to play—at least in the synoptic Gospels. Can we instead better understand his role less in terms of its dependence upon a necessary divine status and more in terms of his desire to *communicate* fullness of life and *empower* people within the community?

Most of the Gospel writers are keen to understand the incarnation of God's re-creative nature in Jesus in terms of Jesus being the *unique* focus of God's redemptive purpose. In this view, Jesus is the savior who is the one to redeem us all by his death; Jesus is the personification of all the flourishing that God desires for humanity. The familiar birth narratives of Matthew and Luke with their complex genealogies and curious descriptions of the conception itself (Mt 1:18; Lk 1:35) and the mysterious prologue of John's Gospel (1:1–14) all work to this purpose. So too does the Gospel writers' use of terms like "Son of God" and "Son of man" to describe Jesus. And in later centuries more complex phrases or creedal statements evolved such as, "very God and very man" or "of one being with the Father" to further articulate something meaningful about the evolving appreciation of Jesus' redemptive purpose as being bound up with and achieved through his dual nature.

But in the earliest of the Gospels *there is no birth narrative.* In Mark there is no attempt to articulate an understanding of the incarnation as "wrought from on high." Mark does, however, have a description of Jesus' baptism. It is here at his baptism that Jesus appears to become aware for the first time of his relationship to God. And it is this moment of awareness on Jesus' part that may serve to provide us with a different reading of what incarnation might mean for all of us.

The synoptics each record that as Jesus emerged from the water, he heard God's voice declaring to him: " 'You are my Son, the Beloved; with you I am well pleased' " (Mk 1:11; see also Mt 3:17, Lk 3:22). This unexpected realization of his connection to God is expressed in the language of "sonship"; from his baptism Jesus understands God to be his Father, the Father who has been absent from the Gospels (except for the birth narratives in Matthew and Luke). Suddenly the rumors, sarcastic comments, and jibes about Jesus' origins and parentage, so familiar from John's Gospel (8:19, 39, 41) fall into place. But whatever the truth about his earthly beginnings, at the moment of his baptism, God speaks directly to Jesus' deep-seated anxiety and sense of disconnection and incompleteness and heals Jesus' wounds.

Immediately afterward in the wilderness Jesus experiences temptation. Trying to come to terms with his new identity, Jesus wrestles with those doubts and inner demons that try to deny and undermine what has been newly revealed:

And the tempter came and said to him, "If you are the Son of God ... All these I will give you, if you will fall down and worship me." (Mt 4:3–9; see also Lk 4:1–13)

We can almost hear the unspoken and subtle implication, the inner voice of doubt aimed at the very root of Jesus' new-sprung hope, tempting him to deny what God has disclosed: "*If you are* the Son of God." The devil wants Jesus to disavow his newly discovered connection to God and acknowledge allegiance to him instead. In other words, "If you will worship me and be *my son*, I will be a better father, more generous, a father who knows what a son really needs." Yet despite this monumental struggle with self-doubt, the forty days in the desert allow Jesus to accept his sonship and experience his essential connection with God. The time in the desert enables Jesus to heal and to become whole as he realizes he is blessed and beloved, incorporated into God's endless generativity and into God's desire that human beings flourish.

The baptism narrative provides an alternative articulation of the meaning of incarnation. The moment of revelation ("You are my Son, the Beloved") in which Jesus acknowledges his connection with God and consents to the possibility that God-is-in-him, offers a different description of what incarnation means and how it operates. The flow of divine creativity is triggered in Jesus by the healing spark of recognition and connection. This healing spark enables Jesus to experience fullness of life within himself and in turn offer that same flourishing to others. And if we understand incarnation to be about *Jesus' recognition of God's presence in his own embodied person*, we can then see how humanity might in turn come to discover, consent to, and partake in divine creativity and receive the Spirit's promised empowerment and fullness of life in whatever way might be best for each of us.

A desire for healing

How does Jesus' bodily presence relate to those occasions when people experience healing? And what happens when Jesus is not physically present at the moment of healing or when healing seems to fail? Is Jesus the all-powerful sole agent of healing, as traditionally understood, or is his function more to empower and to give people permission to open themselves to God, to risk experiencing God's gratuitous re-creative healing in and for themselves?

The healing of the blind man at Bethsaida (Mk 8:22–26) clearly suggests that the man was simply the passive recipient of Jesus' healing power: "Some people brought a blind man to him and begged him to touch him. He took the blind man by the hand and led him out of the village" (8:22–23). This passivity is the characteristic stance of many Gospel healing stories and is reinforced by those occasions when healing fails or when Jesus' disciples need to resort to Jesus. In one story the disciples fail to heal, and the cure only occurs after the boy's father appeals directly to Jesus:

> Just then a man from the crowd shouted, "Teacher, I beg
> you to look at my son; he is my only child. Suddenly a
> spirit seizes him, and all at once he shrieks. It convulses
> him until he foams at the mouth; it mauls him and will
> scarcely leave him. I begged your disciples to cast it out,
> but they could not." (Lk 9:38–40; see also Mk 9:14–18, Mt
> 17:14–16)

Although Jesus heals this boy, were there other occasions when there was no healing? Were there people whom Jesus himself was unable to heal and whose stories were, unsurprisingly, omitted from the Gospels? What about those unable to risk responding to Jesus, for instance, the rich young man?

> He said to him, "Teacher, I have kept all these
> [commandments] since my youth." Jesus, looking at him,

loved him and said, "You lack one thing: go, sell what you own, and give the money to the poor, and you will have treasure in heaven; then come, follow me." When he heard this, he was shocked and went away grieving, for he had many possessions. (Mk 10:20–22)

Perhaps the rich young man came back the next day or after dark. Perhaps the challenge of wholeness, the threat of life, was too much for him. Or perhaps the story is not about whether he had (enough) faith in Jesus' ability to heal him but rather that the young man was not (sufficiently) in need, not yet at a place in his life where he was able to recognize his need for wholeness. Mark and Luke have him ask: "What must I do to *inherit* eternal life?" (Mk 10:17, Lk 18:18, emphasis mine). Perhaps the young man's language reveals that he had already received many inheritances and knew their value, but was now looking for the one that would guarantee ultimate felicity. Was Jesus' response to sell everything and give it to the poor meant to encourage the rich young man to meet people who experienced utter poverty and despair and thereby enable the young man to recognize the real nature of his need?

Maybe the man's lack of wholeness was not just a consequence of a comfortable or an apparently virtuous lifestyle but the weight of unacknowledged psychological distress. Low self-esteem, negative personal image, destructive feelings of unfocused shame, and inferiority prevent us from experiencing what we need to flourish. We lack what will trigger the honest recognition of our need and address our feelings of being incomplete and unfulfilled.

Healing and wholeness can only be willingly embraced; they cannot be forced upon anyone unready or unable to accept it. And because healing springs both from the visceral urge for life and connection to others and out of authentic desolation and despair, perhaps Jesus could not heal when there was no spark of recognition and no experience of need that would allow healing to flow.

Indeed, other healing narratives appear to confirm that Jesus needs a "spark" in order to heal, for instance, the story of the woman cured of hemorrhages:

> She had heard about Jesus, and came up behind him in the crowd and touched his cloak, for she said, "If I but touch his clothes, I will be made well." Immediately her hemorrhage stopped; and she felt in her body that she was healed of her disease. Immediately aware that power had gone forth from him, Jesus turned about in the crowd and said, "Who touched my clothes?" And his disciples said to him, "You can see the crowed pressing in on you; how can you say, 'Who touched me?'" He looked all around to see who had done it. But the woman, knowing what had happened to her, came in fear and trembling, fell down before him, and told him the whole truth. He said to her, "Daughter, your faith has made you well; go in peace, and be healed of your disease." (Mk 5:27–34)

There is a very curious dimension to this story. The woman decides to approach Jesus, saying to herself, "If I but touch his clothes I will be made well." Only after he recognizes that "power had gone forth from him" does Jesus speak and appear to ratify what has already happened, "Daughter, your faith has made you well; go in peace, and be healed." What is happening? What does her preexistent faith, her state of mind, bring to the healing process? Is it possible that the woman has somehow healed herself, and how could this be possible? Or does the bodily presence of Jesus, from whom power had gone forth, hint at something more extraordinary?

The story has much in common with the story about the anonymous Syrophoenician woman whose love for her daughter, her desperation, and her passionate fury at Jesus' initial dismissive response, spill over and appear to carry Jesus out beyond the frontiers of his own experience. For Jesus is left only to declare what has already happened:

> She begged him to cast the demon out of her daughter. He said to her, "Let the children be fed first, for it is not fair to take the children's food and throw it to the dogs." But she answered him, "Sir, even the dogs under the table eat the children's crumbs." Then he said to her, *"For saying that,* you may go—*the demon has left* your daughter." (Mk 7:26–29, emphasis mine)

In a parallel version of this story in Matthew, the woman cries out to Jesus: "'Have mercy on me ...'" and when Jesus ignores her, she kneels directly in front of him, saying: "'Lord, help me'" (Mt 15:22–25). She will not countenance being ignored or dismissed. Her fervent appeal appears to spring out of something in her that wills him to connect and join with her to make her daughter well again. He responds, "'Woman, great is your faith! Let it be done for you as you wish'" (15:28). What sparks from deep within her is her *desire*—a much stronger word than "wish" used in the RSV translation. Her desire is a primal creative energy that wills something to happen and that Jesus senses. The faith that he commends is not so much faith in him, but faith that the thing she passionately wills, if he joins her, will happen.

Likewise, in Luke's account of the cure of a leper it seems that the man with leprosy recognizes something about Jesus and that this instantly moves the man to risk asking for help:

Once, when he was in one of the cities, there was a man
covered with leprosy. When he saw Jesus, he bowed with
his face to the ground and begged him, *"Lord, if you choose,
you can make me clean."* Then Jesus stretched out his hand,
touched him, and said, "I do choose. Be made clean." (Lk
5:12–13, emphasis mine)

Here is a man who is ostracized from society and from physical
interaction with others because of his body; he knew pain and
desperation firsthand. Jesus is the catalyst that triggers the bursting
forth of his desire for re-connection and re-incorporation within
the body of the community; Jesus and the man *both choose* to allow
their shared creative desire to make something happen, and it
does.

Similarly in the story of the healing of the paralyzed man,
friends are united by the deep desire to give back to the paralyzed
man his life within the community:

Just then some men came, carrying a paralyzed man on a
bed. They were trying to bring him in and lay him before
Jesus; but finding no way to bring him in because of the
crowd, they went up on the roof and let him down ....
When he saw their faith, he said, "Friend, your sins are
forgiven you." (Lk 5:18–20, emphasis mine)

In the story of the centurion's servant, the centurion only
needs for Jesus to agree to his desire for healing to occur:

And Jesus went with them, but when he was not far from
the house, the centurion sent friends to say to him, "Lord,
do not trouble yourself ... but only speak the word, and let
my servant be healed. ..." *When Jesus heard this he was*

amazed ... [and] said, "I tell you, not even in Israel have I found such faith." (Lk 7:6–9, emphasis mine)

The blind man at Jericho also follows this same pattern:

As he approached Jericho, a blind man was sitting by the roadside begging. When he heard a crowd going by, he asked what was happening. They told him, "Jesus of Nazareth is passing by." *Then he shouted, "Jesus, Son of David, have mercy on me!"* ... Jesus stood still and ordered the man to be brought to him; and when he came near, he asked him, "What do you want me to do for you?" He said, "Lord, let me see again." Jesus said to him, "Receive your sight; *your faith has saved you.*" (Lk 18:35–42, emphasis mine)

Each of the above stories repeats the same formula:

- The bodily presence of Jesus (however close) evokes an immediate recognition and response on the part of the individuals themselves, their family, or their friends;

- their response (their faith) takes the form of a strong desire to connect with Jesus, even before he has approached or spoken directly to them;

- Jesus and the other individuals, whether they are physically present or simply represented by third parties, actively engage with the moment-at-hand: they *desire* something to happen;

- all parties take risks in opening themselves up to unforeseeable consequences;

- everyone, even the witnesses and Jesus himself, experiences radical amazement at what happens;

- healing, wholeness, and the reincorporation of broken and wounded bodies into society reveals an interdependence and mutuality between Jesus and the others, creating a relationship that transcends the simple dichotomy of "savior" and "saved."

Brokenhearted Jesus

Throughout her highly original study, Rita Nakashima Brock argues that brokenheartedness is the normative condition of humanity and not the "original sinfulness" or "fallenness" of traditional Pauline theology. Brock goes as far as to argue that brokenheartedness lies at the center of the Trinity: God's ceaseless outpouring of newness and ongoing generativity urges connectedness, creative relationships, and reciprocity; God is incomplete without them. Brock believes that because this condition of brokenheartedness is both natural and inevitable for humanity, made in the image of God, it follows that Jesus himself experienced being incomplete and disconnected.

Brock describes Jesus' earthly ministry as unfolding through a series of encounters in which his bodily presence empowers others to acknowledge their own brokenheartedness and thereby allows healing to happen. She believes that the bodily presence of others allows Jesus to mediate a flourishing and to birth new life and new beginnings. Brock talks in terms of the *erotic power* ("erotic" in the sense of primal or visceral) that exists and flows between Jesus and those who have dared claim wholeness for themselves. She writes that the disciples, those who were all once radically dispossessed and alienated by the Law, gather around Jesus and form a "Christic community" of hope. This community refuses to let Jesus go at his crucifixion, and ultimately holds on to him in death. It is a community that:

restores ... the hope of wholeness ... by not letting go of their
relationships to each other and not letting Jesus' death be
the end of their community. ... [They] refused to let death
defeat them. In taking heart they remembered his presence
and affirmed divine power among them. The resurrection
provided a way for Jesus to continue to live in them, and for
them to live with and for each other. (Brock 100)

This reflection is an extraordinarily powerful idea that has
considerable overlap with the above reading of the healing stories
and suggests that it is too simplistic to see Jesus as the unique
savior figure, who alone is sole possessor of healing power over the
wounded bodies of others. Something else is going on, something
very reminiscent of the power symbolized by the fire that burns the
bush without consuming it. These healings reveal that God uses
power differently from other gods. There is a mutually creative
covenant at the heart of the bond between God and the people.
This covenant allows people a way of getting on the inside of a
relationship with God. And this covenant commits God to
responding to each moment of crisis-opportunity by cooperating
with people to bring healing, justice, and renewed flourishing into
the world. God invites people to share in the task of giving shape
to the ongoing work of creation.

A community of passionate outcasts

Besides Jesus, others are involved in the healing stories, others
who are just as passionate as he is, sometimes perhaps even more
passionate for what is just and right. (Think of his initial rejection
of the Syrophoenician woman.) An extraordinary community of
social outcasts is drawn to Jesus. These outcasts are those who
recognized their own wounds and encountered the regenerative
power of God incarnate in human bodies through Jesus' bodily

presence. A community is formed that can use its experience of Jesus as the touchstone for the release of the creative energy that brings healing.

For example, in the story of the woman with the hemorrhage, her visceral desire (she has absolutely nothing more to lose) for healing and for the restoration of her body to the community calls forth a response from Jesus. When Jesus is described as being aware that power had gone forth from him, what is really happening is that God's re-creative energy is released and flows *both ways* between them. Similarly, in the story of the healing of the widow of Nain's son (Lk 7:11–17), Jesus recognizes the mother's absolute brokenness. His "compassion for her" (7:13) calls forth and urges from both of them, and from God, the creative response of restoration of life to her son.

The same mutually creative covenant at work at Jesus' baptism and amidst these once brokenhearted individuals is the manifest sign of the God who ever draws people into new life, even when life appears to be at the point of collapse. When Jesus hung in despair upon the cross, aware only of his impending death, his life-sustaining connection to his God and his Father ("My God, *my* God") held God to the covenant. The covenant that guarantees God's commitment to us, whatever may happen in life or in death. And God makes the most extraordinary response to this covenant in the form of that gratuitous outpouring of re-creative loving that is what we call "resurrection."

For God's resurrection of Jesus is the proof needed by the community (now as much as then) that God will not be bound by anything other than an enduring and infinite love for creation. God will always respond empathically, creatively, and with outrageous love to all who risk opening themselves up to the "yet-more" of God and to the reality of the limitations of human life and their need for mutuality, wholeness, and connection with the rest of creation.

Such are the people who have risked facing their own brokenness and have come to experience for themselves what it means to be embodied human beings freed into flourishing. Such is the community that sustains Jesus in his ministry, embodying for him and mirroring back to him, the life-giving energy of the human heart healed by the ever regenerative power of God. Such is the community of the nameless men and women who co-create with Jesus relationships of mutual trust that break asunder the old dynamics of power, gender, and social control, and who are able to birth a radically new vision of divine abundance and fruitfulness. Such is the community that seeks to enable people to live in the flourishing fullness of God's ever re-creative power. This community is what the church is meant to be.

Time to think about your own experience

In a time of silence you may now wish to consider your answers to the following questions. If you are with others in a group you may choose to share your responses with them.

- What is your experience of having or being a body? When and how has your body flourished? Given the state of your body now, how do you experience God and God's blessing in and through it?

- What do you find more meaningful or appealing: the idea of salvation or of flourishing? Why is this? Which is more important, life before death or life after death?

- Have you ever prayed for healing or wholeness? What exactly was it that you wanted? Why do you think God does not seem to answer the prayers of some people?

■   What are your thoughts and feelings about Jesus' healing
     encounters? What do you think of the idea that that Jesus'
     disciples worked with God to bring him back from the
     dead?

Flourishing and the Body of Christ

Jesus' first followers, once a disparate group of individuals united
by the common experience of touching and being physically
touched by Jesus, became a more clearly defined fellowship with
distinct beliefs, values, and practices. In the first decades following
Jesus' death, the disciples gained a new self-awareness that came to
be identified and labeled as "Christian." A distinct community was
born: the church.

It is significant that very early in its history, the church lost
interest in the relationship between healing and the proclamation
of the good news of the kingdom, so central to Jesus' ministry and
so often the context of his preaching. The healing miracles were
gradually regarded only as a source of incontrovertible evidence for
the divinity of Jesus. The substantive meaning of incarnation
withdrew from the realm of the physical world and physical bodies
and became merely an idea, a tenet of belief. The incarnation was
the intellectual prerequisite to understanding Jesus' birth and
ministry. And even these became subservient to the great fact of
his saving death. Jesus' death was seen, in Western Christendom at
least, as the real purpose of his earthly existence.

And while the church continued to teach that people were
made in the image and likeness of God, humanity's "fall," brought
about through the temptations of the flesh (understood to be

perpetuated by sexual reproduction) meant that the physical body came to represent all that was sinful and all that should be beaten down into submission (1 Cor 9:27). As a result, the body ceased to signify the real, fleshly, physical body of real human beings and became instead a parody of itself.

The Body of Christ

At the resurrection and the ascension Jesus' physical body disappeared and allowed the notion of the Body of Christ to signify a different reality. The physical nature of Christ's body was transformed into a metaphor for the church: an abstract, institutionalized and therefore gendered and hierarchical body, whose members were regulated by the disciplines of right belief and action. And after the Ascension the only way that God could be present in a body was if that body was the church.

The idea of the church as the Body of Christ has its roots in the synoptic accounts of the Last Supper. Jesus took bread and wine, declared them to be his body and blood and commanded his followers to share this meal in remembrance of him (Lk 22:17–20). Those who shared bread with Jesus—here, as at other times in his ministry—became a fellowship of "companions" or "bread eaters." And although Jesus himself never used the term "body" to describe this relationship (indeed it is unclear whether he ever intended to establish an institutionalized church as distinct from the wandering community that gathered around him) the continuing practice of this table fellowship and the idea of a shared identity around the breaking of bread was ripe for transformation by Paul into that great extended metaphor of the body found in 1 Corinthians 12 and Romans 12.

For Paul the idea of the church as the *body* of Christ means exactly that: the church is a living organism, a body, whose various members together form the parts of a greater body:

For just as the body is one and has many members, and all
the members of the body, though many, are one body, so it
is with Christ. For in the one Spirit we were baptized into
one body …. Indeed, the body does not consist of one
member but of many. If the foot would say, "Because I am
not a hand, I do not belong to the body," that would not
make it any less a part of the body. And if the ear would
say, "Because I am not an eye, I do not belong to the
body," that would not make it any less a part of the body.
If the whole body were an eye, where would the hearing
be? If the whole body were hearing, where would the sense
of smell be? But, as it is, God arranged the members in the
body, each one of them, as he chose. If all were a single
member, where would the body be? As it is there are many
members, yet one body. The eye cannot say to the hand, "I
have no need of you," nor again the head to the feet, "I
have no need of you." On the contrary, the members of
the body that seem to be weaker are indispensable, and
those members of the body that we think less honorable
we clothe with greater honor, and our less respectable
members are treated with greater respect; whereas our
more respectable members do not need this. But God has
so arranged the body, giving the greater honor to the
inferior member, that there may be no dissension within
the body, but the members may have the same care for
one another. If one member suffers, all suffer together with
it; if one member is honored, all rejoice together with it.
Now you are the body of Christ and individually members
of it. (1 Cor 12:12–27)

For Paul becoming a Christian implies taking on a new identity
and allowing the needs of an individual's physical body to be

subsumed into the greater Body of Christ, where there is embodied (literally and metaphorically) a radical equivalency between all members. In the Body of Christ the needs of all members must be recognized and met in order for the whole body to function healthily and to flourish. The original context for Paul's rhetoric may have been dissension in the community about status or function, for instance, about a person's place at the table or if the community could contemplate slaves having parity with owners. The notion of equivalency directly addresses dissension and enacts the extraordinary idea that the weak are indispensable, that the Body of Christ, as a radically unique community bearing the subversive memory of Jesus and his prophetic ministry, actively needs the weak, despised, and outcast in order to worthily bear the name of Christ.

This same radical idea is found in Paul's letter to the Romans and suggests what must have been the astonishing (and for some, deeply threatening) sight of individuals from the lowest ranks called by God to exercise ministry and leadership within the worshipping community. This radically new social reality of the Body of Christ was one where the grace given by God overturns socially acquired authority and privilege:

> For as in one body we have many members, and not all the members have the same function, so we, who are many, are one body in Christ, and individually we are members one of another. We have gifts that differ according to the grace given to us …. Let love be genuine … love one another with mutual affection. (Rom 12:4–6, 9–10)

This new form of dynamic between individuals: cross-cultural, boundary-breaking, challenging practices around gender and disability, was the innovative, creative, and practical expression of

God's vision for human flourishing, fragile though it was and riven with the inevitable tensions that accompany any radical social experiment. The topsy-turvy reign of God was embodied, imperfectly and provisionally, in a community drawn together to share bread and celebrate the birthing of astonishing new and holistic ways of remodeling human kinship.

Yet the idea of the church as the Body of Christ may not be the universal, timeless panacea we believe it to be. The idea of a "body" suggests that growth and flourishing demand a willing recognition of interdependence, relationality, equivalency, and complementarity of function. The concept of the Body of Christ, however, does nothing to change the *actual status* of those viewed to be inferior or to be the less respectable members. A slave is still a slave, and an armpit is still an armpit.

The idea of the church as the Body of Christ is, notwithstanding Christian rhetoric, one premised on hierarchies of power and function, on gender and status. Despite the images of joyful sharing between believers in Acts 4–5, it is clear from the way Paul needs to address dissension in the early Roman church that the body metaphor itself failed to promote the dissolution of the fundamental binary divisions of the day, even between those living "in Christ." Indeed this metaphor could not but maintain the reality of the lived social hierarchies: who wants to volunteer to be an inferior member? The Body of Christ is a metaphor that ultimately fails to re-image true social transformation and flourishing.

The vine and the branches

John's Gospel, however, memorably records Jesus himself comparing his relationship with his companions with that of a vine and its fruiting branches:

"I am the true vine, and my Father is the vinegrower. ...
Abide in me as I abide in you. Just as the branch cannot
bear fruit by itself unless it abides in the vine, neither can
you unless you abide in me. I am the vine, you are the
branches. Those who abide in me and I in them bear much
fruit." (Jn 15:1, 4–5)

Just as Jesus the vine is sustained by God the vine grower, so
all those who remain together in fellowship with Jesus, those who
abide in Jesus like the many branches all connected to and
sustained by the vine itself, will thrive, grow, and be green and
fruitful. This text is an important link with the language of
flourishing from the Hebrew Scripture. The vine metaphor
provides a description of how the regenerative power of God
results in flourishing and fruitfulness for all. All the branches are
equal (there are no inferior or less respectable branches), and all
branches equally and without distinction can bear fruit. There is
no hierarchy to excuse or to condemn the various branches.

A vine is in many ways a more powerful metaphor for the
nature of the church than that of a body. Like the body metaphor,
the vine maintains Jesus' radical notion that relationship is
essential to the well-being of the whole, but the vine image goes
beyond the language of the body, which has an inherent functional
hierarchy because some parts of the body are "more respectable"
and others are "inferior." The vine metaphor presents *the
transformative possibility of fruitfulness and flourishing* for each
member of the inclusive community and articulates a new vision of
divine abundance as well as a new way of being in the world.

The church and human flourishing

Unfortunately many experience the church as a place in which
decent people feel profoundly uncomfortable and embarrassed.

Many experience the church as a place that has an unwholesome preoccupation with individual acts of sin, while ignoring the cumulative effects of its own teachings: the inculcation of chronic and unacknowledged guilt and shame. Many experience the church as a place where human brokenness and darkness are addressed solely and superficially by the clichéd exhortation to "repent and turn to the light of Christ." Many experience a church that fails to explore human brokenness and darkness creatively and fails to discover those unforeseen and precious treasures that might guide human wisdom and promote healing and flourishing.

When Paul talks about those parts of the Body of Christ that are "less honorable," uncomely, or shameful and that need to be covered up and hidden (1 Cor 12:23), he exposes a level of unspoken or even unacknowledged guilt and shame. And this shame and guilt is reinforced by the traditional teaching about fig leaves and the taint of an unfocused sinfulness passed on (allegedly) by those acts of sexual expression and procreation with which most of humanity is engaged.

In some church communities, these feelings are then buttressed by the widespread practice of personal or congregational confession that is an intrinsic part of preparation for worship. This practice requires people to spend the little time allowed in the liturgy for silent reflection in rooting around in the recesses of their minds for something to confess, effectively encouraging a sense of unworthiness. Feelings of unfocused and undefined shamefulness can eat away at integrity, the sense of individual value and personal fitness to receive and participate in the Eucharist. This kind of confession seems to fly in the face of Jesus' practice of inviting everyone to eat together and share unconditionally in a community of inclusive belonging, fruitfulness, and flourishing.

While there are some of us who *do* come to church with things we genuinely need to confess, most of us come conditioned to the fact that we will have to confess something. And while it is good to periodically question ourselves and our values, nevertheless, we accommodate ourselves to a habit of collusion by confessing acts of superficial wrongdoing while rarely articulating those deeper issues that compound guilt into destructive and corrosive shame. Consequently this practice of superficial confession causes many practicing Christians, as well as those who do not generally come to church or who have ceased to attend, to fail to find in the church any positive, resonant sense of relevance, or any meaning rooted in their actual lived experience or need. They fail to find much, if any, space or opportunity to articulate and explore what it means to live this one life fully and abundantly.

The church has lost its sense of being called to be a practicing ("operating" and "still imperfect") community of trustworthiness and transformation. And as long as fruitfulness, for individuals as well as for communities, remains a forgotten purpose and challenge of fellowship in Christ, as long as the church fails to live the fullness of its calling to embody and promote human flourishing, it will not be reckoned worthy of the trust of those among whom it seeks to minister. It is clear that the metaphors of both "the body" and "the vine" have proven to be challenges to turn into reality. Indeed, if we ask if the church is faithful to its calling to be a place of flourishing for all people, we may struggle to answer affirmatively.

A theology of flourishing

Jesus told his disciples that he "came that they may have life, and have it abundantly" (Jn 10:10). Life in abundance, flourishing, suggests healing, wholeness, and a process of radical openness to the disclosure of new possibilities for individuals, for the community, and for the world. Flourishing lies at the heart of the original mandate given by Jesus to his first followers. But where is a theology of flourishing? Can the church be a place of flourishing, and what might that mean? Can the church be a place of healing and wholeness where the false dualisms and divisions found in our social order are exposed and where inclusiveness is practiced? Can the church ever become a community that dares to challenge slavish conformity to the past for the sake of an honest quest for truthfulness in lived experience? Can the church once more speak to peoples' deepest needs and aspirations and mediate God's regenerative love in the world?

A theology of flourishing must be distinguished from a theology that expects the perfectibility of human life. To flourish and to be whole is not to live in or to strive for some perfect state of existence. The church teaches that the Christian life is about accepting Jesus to be the *way out* of this sinful life into righteous living, the *way back* to that lost paradise in Eden, and the *way into* eternal life. In contrast, a theology of flourishing embraces human imperfection and contingency and emphasizes the primacy of natality: of life lived to the full, from new beginning to new beginning in the face of our inevitable physical demise and in openness to the "yet-more" of God.

A theology of flourishing requires us to question traditional theologies based on notions of divine omnipotence and omniscience and notions of human "fallen-ness." A theology of flourishing requires us to accept that the limitations of human existence are normal and natural—indeed that the limitations are precisely where God is revealed. A theology of flourishing requires a church willing to *celebrate all that constitutes human existence*, rather than constantly bemoaning and lamenting the ways humans fall short.

The mission of the church

If the church is to become like that first community around Jesus, a community of trustworthiness and transformative practice, then its central task is to rediscover and exercise a theology of flourishing and fullness of life. The first followers discovered that in facing their own brokenheartedness, they were able to experience flourishing and able to speak effectively and trustworthily to their contemporaries. Today's church must listen with ever-renewed attention to the "speaking-creating" voice of God and then proclaim the great good news of unconditional love for everyone. The church must learn how to demonstrate to the world its rejection of the ways of death and how to practice a gospel of natality, fruitfulness, and flourishing.

Living the Gospel requires a commitment to rediscovering and emulating Jesus' habit of a transgressive reading of the Law. Living the Gospel requires a commitment to reshaping the embodied pastoral practices of the church in order to enable spiritual growth for all who seek to follow Jesus. The church needs a theology both rooted in and inseparable from an embodied and holistic pastoral practice, a pastoral practice that does not prefer or create false dichotomies between what is written or revealed and lived experience.

In order to preach and practice a Gospel of fruitfulness and flourishing for all, the church itself needs to be broken open. Perhaps the breaking of the Body of Christ, central to the liturgical life of the church, needs to be experienced by the institution itself. If the church is to rediscover what it means to be reenergized by the regenerative spirit of God, it must undergo being wounded, pierced, and torn asunder. Then its life, calling, and witness will once again become authoritative and compelling.

Is it possible that the regenerative power of the physical body of Jesus, his ability to connect creatively with the bodies of others, might be restored to the body of believers called church? Can this Body of Christ, this fruitful vine that is Jesus and his followers, flourish, and God's re-creative life-giving energy flow through it again? Can such a thing even be imagined?

The establishment figures of Jesus' day judged his teaching, miracles, and healing to be profoundly blasphemous. Jesus flouted religious categories and practices, divided opinion as to their origin and purpose, thwarted the expectations of all who witnessed them, and opened the social and religious order to the radical newness of God's re-creative and regenerative action. Jesus' physical body and the physical bodies of other people became the location for God's self-revelation and for the embodiment of the good news of the kingdom of heaven.

The time is right for the church to rediscover how to read Scripture subversively and with imagination. The time is right for the church to take its lead from Jesus and risk the possibility of letting go of some deeply held convictions and assumptions in order to find itself in a new place, empowered and emboldened to be a more inclusive, authentic, and creative community for the healing and flourishing of the world.

Time to think about your own experience

In a time of silence you may now wish to consider your answers to the following questions.If you are with others in a group you may choose to share your responses with them.

- How do you understand the church? What are the strengths and weaknesses in comparing it with the "body" of Christ or with a "vine"?

- When have you reflected on your own incompleteness or lack of fulfillment? Is incompleteness a better description for human existence than the language of sinfulness and imperfection? Why or why not?

■ What sorts of things might prevent your church from being a place where people find fullness of life? How might it be possible for the church to transform its pastoral practice? How could you help create that transformation?

■ Before beginning to read the next chapter, spend time exploring what you feel about imagination. Do you have imagination? If someone is called an imaginative person, is that a compliment or not? How do you feel about using imagination to read the Bible?

Jesus, Scripture,
and Risk-shaped Imagination

There are two common assumptions among Christians. The first is that prophecy is foretelling the future and predicting God's plan. The second is that there is no place for the imagination in the "serious business" of reading Scripture, doing theology, or living a moral and spiritual life (because the imagination undermines rationality and encourages escape from reality into the dangerous realms of the fanciful). A careful reading of any Hebrew prophet, however, demonstrates that neither of these assumptions is correct.

Jeremiah (see Chapter Four), for example, does not foretell the future—how could he? God surprises everyone with a last-minute change of heart and the future turns out very different from Jeremiah's expectations. Jeremiah uses words, actions, and symbols to confront people with God's perception of reality, to rouse them from their sleep-walking. He awakens them to the dissonance between where they are and where they need to be in order to flourish. Prophets are the bearers of unwelcome truth. They deliberately upset people by demanding that they think again and imagine the "yet-more" of God, the what-is-not-but-might-be, the newness whose precise nature and shape is uncertain and beyond sight yet also sure and promised. Imagination goes hand in hand with prophecy.

The tool of imagination

Imagination involves paradigm shifting, altering perceptions of reality, in order to recognize God in what is completely inconceivable a moment before it happens. Think of Sarah and Abraham's conception of Isaac, Moses before the burning bush, and Jeremiah when God set aside the Law for the sake of the relationship with the people. God is not like other gods; God's ways are altogether different from any other god. God is not content with the ordinary, easy metaphors of divinity, predictably omnipotent and omniscient, an "either-or" god with an insider-outsider, saved-or-damned mentality. God refuses to be confined within the expected outcomes, physical limitations, or possibilities of language and thought. Further, because God is beyond all knowing and can only be spoken about metaphorically, *the imagination is an essential tool* when it comes to both a rich and critical discernment of the what-has-been-revealed and being unreservedly open to the what-might-next-be-revealed. But imagination always comes risk-shaped, for it demands openness to fresh thinking. And imagination is crucial for doing theology; the theologian or preacher who is unable to use his or her imagination will be unable to articulate much of value.

God is hidden within the texts of Scripture without being confined by or reduced to any once-and-for-all readings. Moreover, Scripture is capable of holding the possibilities for multiple disclosures of God's voice at different times and in different contexts. We must discover how to use our imagination if we are ever to free ourselves from the habit of trying to "force fresh lives into old narratives" (a phrase of Walter Brueggemann's, I believe). We must remain open to the adventure of new revelation in texts that we have largely forfeited to stale familiarity and indifferent neglect.

It would be mistaken, however, to think that the use of imagination is something particularly novel or newfangled or something peculiar to that phase of human development called post-modernity. Imagination has always been a player in the writing, editing, translation, and communication of Scripture. How could it not have been? Those taught to believe the Bible to be "the inerrant Word of God" or that Scripture is to a greater or lesser extent inspired by the Spirit, need to recognize that the imagination is the bit of the human psyche that is most readily open to the action of the Spirit. The imagination is the interface between Spirit and human psyche; the action of the Spirit in human intuition is identical to the working of the imagination in that it encourages, prompts, and enthuses ideas and words, texts and interpretations, individual prayer and community action, radical truth-telling and astonishing justice-making. But how is imagination used in relationship to Scripture? To answer this, first we will explore how Jesus deals with Scripture, how the Gospel writers handled texts, and finally, how the business of reading and interpreting the Bible engages with individuals, communities, and the planet that sustains us all.

Jesus and Scripture

Central to Jesus' ministry is his transgressive interpretation of the Law and the Prophets. His decision, for instance, to take a portion from Isaiah's prophecy and apply it to himself (Lk 4:16–30) at first provoked surprise and then offense in his local congregation when people finally realized the full implication of his words. Throughout his ministry, Jesus' actions and words confront assumptions about the meaning of Scripture and the normative interpretations of the Law. On one occasion Jesus questions whether it is permissible or not to pluck grain to eat while walking as, "'David did when he and his companions were hungry'" (Lk 6:3). On another occasion, in the course of healing a man with a withered hand (Mk 3:1–6), Jesus challenges the Pharisees' interpretation of the nature and purpose of the Sabbath and invites debate about the very meaning and value of the Law itself.

While on this last occasion the Pharisees decline the opportunity to dispute with him, there are others times in which the Pharisees and lawyers "cross-examine him about many things, lying in wait for him, to catch him in something he might say" (Lk 11:53–54). Debate appears to be precisely Jesus' intention. Jesus wants to open up an imaginative—and uncomfortable—discussion about the significance and function of the Law, about whether or not certain interpretations of the Law serve to connect people with God or come between them and God, about whether or not the Law's power, its moral force, constrains people in conformity or frees them into flourishing. This debate occurs throughout Jesus' ministry. In the story of the woman taken in adultery, for instance, Jesus confronts the use of the Law as a weapon:

> "Teacher, this woman was caught in the very act of committing adultery. Now in the law Moses commanded us to stone such women. Now what do you say?" They said this to test him, so that they might have some charge to bring against him. ... When they kept on questioning him, he straightened up and said to them, "Let anyone among you who is without sin be the first to throw a stone at her." (Jn 8:4–7)

In the story of the Sabbath healing of the crippled woman the debate appears again:

> But the Lord answered him and said, "You hypocrites! Does not each of you on the sabbath untie his ox or his donkey from the manger, and lead it away to give it water? And ought not this woman, a daughter of Abraham whom Satan bound for eighteen long years, be set free from this bondage on the sabbath day?" (Lk 13:15–16)

In the story of the cure of the man with dropsy Jesus
challenges the religious leaders:

> And Jesus asked the lawyers and Pharisees, "Is it lawful to
> cure people on the sabbath, or not?" But they were silent.
> So Jesus took him and healed him, and sent him away.
> Then he said to them, "If one of you has a child or an ox
> that has fallen into a well, will you not immediately pull it
> out on a sabbath day?" And they could not reply to this.
> (Lk 14:3–6)

The constant probing about the meaning of the Sabbath and
what Sabbath activities are acceptable not only raises the issue of
what activities honor God, the Lord of the Sabbath, but also raises
questions about our very understanding of God's nature. Does God
have the Pharisees' legalistic approach to the covenant? Or is God,
instead, very different than a superficial interpretation of the Law
might suggest? Do some interpretations of the Law do a radical
injustice to God's original intentions?

Jesus fuels this debate by insisting that people reconsider their
assumptions when reading Scripture and how their interpretations
may impact others. In addition, Jesus reveals through his public
actions and his relationships an alternative interpretation of the
Law. Specifically, by deliberately restoring those on the *outside* of
the Law to the *inside*, Jesus constructs an imaginative bridge to
new and inclusive readings that subvert the insider-outsider matrix
and turn upside down the normative assumptions about God and
the nature of God's relationship with people.

Jesus' proclamation of this inclusive kingdom of God is an
astonishingly radical and risky act of imagination. For its starting
place, Jesus' imaginative proclamation invariably begins with
everyday stories about the way the Law impacts ordinary people:

"Teacher, tell my brother to divide the family inheritance with me." But he said to him, "Friend, who set me to be a judge or arbitrator over you?" And he said to them, "Take care! Be on your guard against all kinds of greed; for one's life does not consist in the abundance of possessions." Then he told them a parable: "The land of a rich man produced abundantly. And he thought to himself, 'What should I do, for I have no place to store my crops?' Then he said, 'I will do this: I will pull down my barns and build larger ones, and there I will store all my grain and my goods. And I will say to my soul, "Soul, you have ample goods laid up for many years; relax, eat, drink, be merry."' But God said to him, 'You fool! This very night your life is being demanded of you. And the things you have prepared, whose will they be?' So it is with those who store up treasures for themselves but are not rich toward God." (Lk 12:13–21)

At one level this encounter is about a man who, perceiving Jesus to be a popular rabbi and interpreter of the Law, requests a judgment about a pressing legal matter. Jesus' response is brief. He is not concerned with the Law as a system of judicial decisions. Instead he tells the story about a successful man of property. Jesus not only invites his questioner to find a solution through a leap of his imagination as he engages with the parable, Jesus opens up a window of imagination that throws light on the bigger picture of the relationship between the Law and the true nature of God's kingdom.

Jesus' imaginative technique is well illustrated by this parable. The story is in three parts. First, Jesus articulates a storyline that is consonant with the experience and expectations of his listeners: "The land of a rich man produced abundantly. And ... he said, 'I will pull down my barns and build larger ones, and there I will store all my grain and my goods. And I will ... relax, eat, drink, be merry' " (Lk 12:16–19). Who could disagree with the storyline so far? The listeners are carried along by the flow until suddenly comes the unexpected twist that overturns the anticipated, logical, outcome and confounds the listeners: "But God said to him, 'You fool! This very night your life is being demanded of you. And the things you have prepared, whose will they be?' " (12:20). Finally, the punch line creates a new perspective, a new starting place for understanding the covenant and interpreting the Law, and a new way of imagining and embodying human living and flourishing: " 'So it is with those who store up treasures for themselves but are not rich toward God' " (12:21).

This three-part structure illustrates Jesus' risk-shaped parabolic imagination: a storyline, its disintegration, and then the storyline's resolution, which moves the listeners into a new place of understanding. Jesus' storytelling is a dialectical movement of orientation, disorientation, and reorientation, or to put it in more descriptive language, a kind of narrative journey: a setting out, a going East, a collapse, a going West, before finally arriving home by an unexpected route as a changed person.

Time and again Jesus encourages his listeners to use their imaginations to gain insight into the nature of God. The kingdom of God is like ... a mustard seed, leaven in bread dough, a hidden treasure, a fishing net, a lost coin, a marriage feast, a good Samaritan, a prodigal son, a sower sowing seed. And Jesus constantly urges his listeners: " 'Let anyone with ears to hear listen' " (Mk 4:9). The kingdom of God is a totally new reality that is accessible only by a childlike curiosity, wonder, and imagination, hence Jesus' warning that, "whoever does not receive the kingdom of God as a little child will never enter it" (10:15).

The Gospel writers and Scripture

The breathtakingly radical nature of what Jesus is asking people to do is apparent in the treatment of the parable of the sower:

"Listen! A sower went out to sow. And as he sowed, some seed fell on the path, and the birds came and ate it up. Other seed fell on rocky ground, where it did not have much soil, and it sprang up quickly, since it had no depth of soil. And when the sun rose, it was scorched; and since it had no root, it withered away. Other seed fell among thorns, and the thorns grew up and choked it, and it yielded no grain. Other seed fell into good soil and brought forth grain, growing up and increasing and yielding thirty and sixty and a hundredfold." And he said, "Let anyone with ears to hear listen!" (Mk 4:3–9; see also Mt 13:3–9, Lk 8:5–8)

In this parable Jesus asks his listeners to understand that God works in the world like a sower in the field. While this image is an image that Jesus' listeners recognize and understand immediately, he is actually asking them to consider much more than what sort of soil they are or what yield they have given. Indeed, Jesus asks them to do much more than think about whether or not they have been fruitful or been blessed. Jesus asks his listeners to imagine the radical possibility that God sows blessings like the sower sows seed—indiscriminately, abundantly, extravagantly. Jesus asks his listeners to open their hearts and minds to the discovery that God blesses everyone.

There is support for this interpretation. The early church toned down this outrageous reading by adding a definitive interpretation of this parable. In the church's interpretation, the seed that fell on the path and was eaten up by birds becomes a metaphor for those who are soon lured from the path by the devil, the seed on rocky ground represents those who give up the moment the going gets tough, the seed among thorns are those who are seduced by the fleeting cares and attractions of the world, and only the seed that fell into good soil and brought forth grain represents the committed believer (Mk 4:13–20; see also Mt 13:18–23, Lk 8:11–15).

The desire to turn the parable into an allegory of salvation, the need to eliminate the possibility of multiple interpretations and to neutralize the open-ended, "If you have ears to hear, then hear" tag with its emphasis on individual discernment, speaks of a church that cannot bear to hear the news that God's love is inclusive and that God desires flourishing for all. This interpretation of the parable reveals a church that needs to maintain clear boundaries between those inside the community and those outside of it, a church that needs to build a concrete and distinct identity by narrative closure. There are no more alternative readings. There is only a desire for doctrinal certainty that reduces God's subversive novelty into an exclusive and preferential love for those who belong and conform.

In the Gospels there is a tension between the drive to conformity and closure (through the narrowing of the boundaries of communal textual interpretation) and imaginative and subversive textual readings. This tension is visible in the way the evangelists set their narratives within the broader tradition of Jewish scriptural reading and interpretation. An example of particular interest is the development of the miraculous bread motif woven through the Gospels.

The feeding of the five thousand (Mk 6:32–44; see also Mt 14:13–21, Lk 9:10–17) and the feeding of the four thousand (Mk 8:1–10; see also Mt 15:32–39) are very closely related. These texts may, in fact, be different accounts of the same memory that were already linked with one another before Mark and Matthew (unlike Luke) separated them into two apparently distinct events. (A further, probably independent, version is recounted in John 6:1–14, which is developed into the long and well-known "bread of life" discourse [6:25–40] in which Jesus, according to one possible translation, declares himself to be "the bread of life" [6:35]. In the synoptics the bread of life becomes, instead, associated with the Last Supper narratives: "This is my body." [Mk 14:22, Mt 26:26, Lk 22:19] and the institution of the Eucharist.)

Only John's version of the feeding story (6:31–32) has any theological link to the Hebrew Scripture and to the story of the feeding of the Israelites in the desert (Ex 16:4–36). This lack of connection is surprising in itself, but what is fascinating is that there is no reference, in any of the Gospels, to a story from the Hebrew Scripture that has such obvious and fundamental connection with the Gospel narratives of feeding multitudes:

> A man came from Baal-shalishah, bringing food from the first fruits to the man of God: twenty loaves of barley and fresh ears of grain in his sack. Elisha said, "Give it to the people and let them eat." But his servant said, "How can I set this before a hundred people?" So he repeated, "Give it to the people and let them eat, for thus says the LORD, 'They shall eat and have some left.'" He set it before them, they ate, and had some left, according to the word of the LORD. (2 Kings 4:42–44)

There seems little to account for the lack of connection between this story and the Gospel accounts of miraculous feeding. Why? One reason might be possible questions in the early church about whether the stories of the feeding are somehow inauthentic or less potent in the light of this earlier Elisha narrative. Is the church concerned whether or not the feeding happened precisely as the Gospel writers describe? Does Jesus merely imitate Elisha, to demonstrate that the same God was at work in both stories? Could (or should) Jesus be understood to be necessarily greater than Elisha? These questions misunderstand the textual associations through which Jesus, like the Pharisees and their interpretation of the Law, *actually invites* (or even perhaps demands) imaginative connection-making so as to promote authentic engagement with the business of discovering truth and making meaning.

Midrash and imagination

For some people, of course, the simple answer to the relationship between the Hebrew (Old Testament) and Christian (New Testament) Scriptures and, for instance, between the story of Elisha and that of Jesus, is manifestly one of prophecy. Jesus simply fulfills or perfects what was done in the past in order to show the truth about himself. For others, however, the association is more creative: not prophecy, but *midrash*. Midrash (from the Hebrew verb *daresh*: "to penetrate or burrow within" a text, or else "tease out and go in pursuit of" meaning) is a way of reading Scripture, a mode of interpretation or a relationship between texts and the readers or the community, in which the texts themselves elicit meaning.

Midrash assumes that Scripture is divine speech (the Word of God), that Scripture originates in the mind of God; that it is inerrant, even in apparent textual errors and omissions, and contains nothing redundant. Midrash is a way of reading that, working within communally accepted limits, uses the imagination as the prime interpretive instrument. Midrash prevents an easy over-familiarity with the narrative and the foreclosing of meaning by opening the texts to new and plural interpretations with diverse points of entry and engagement. Midrash holds that Scripture's meanings are multiple and can be drawn out or pursued through the text as the need for meaning arises within the community. In reference to the stories of Elisha and Jesus, meaning and relevance are there to be discovered or teased out through the manifold imaginative connections that might be made by individuals and communities in search of God's truth.

Midrashic reading promotes a richness of textual association that demands a close attention to the reading, the courage to be open to novelty and difference, and the willingness to risk taking a mental leap in order to encounter God as both "revealed" and "yet-hidden" within the texts. Midrashic reading explores a text's gaps and silences. The reader moves back and forth between the gaps and the silences, comparing and contrasting, questioning and answering, seeking out and proclaiming, and weaving a tapestry from the meanings that arise and are called forth by the Spirit that inspires all Scripture.

The Gospels themselves are fundamentally midrashic in nature and structure. They offer us an arrangement of texts that requires us to move backward and forward between the disciples' articulation of the experience of the resurrected Jesus and the memory of his words and deeds as he went about his earthly ministry. This is an important but often unrecognized point. The Gospels proceed *as if* they are telling the story of Jesus from birth through death to resurrection; in fact, the starting point is always the experience of Jesus' resurrection. For the accounts of what "preceded" his resurrection are always told through the lens of resurrection. This means in effect that the Gospels are written both backward, with the resurrection illuminating each memory of what had gone before and forward, as each memory and story anticipates what is known but still to be disclosed.

This "backward-forward" process accounts for those moments

when the evangelists must prevent the story from "getting ahead of itself" and disclosing too much, those episodes, for instance, traditionally explained by reference to a "Messianic secret" (Mk 8:27–30; see also Mt 16:13–20, Lk 9:18–22) and those curious occasions when the same narrative appears both "before" and "after" the accounts of the resurrection. For instance, here is a narrative (unique to Luke) placed at the opening of Jesus' ministry:

> Once while Jesus was standing beside the lake of Gennesaret … he saw two boats there at the shore of the lake; the fishermen had gone out of them and were washing their nets. He got into one of the boats, the one belonging to Simon, and asked him to put out a little way from the shore. Then he taught the crowds from the boat. When he had finished speaking, he said to Simon, "Put out into the deep water and let down your nets for a catch." Simon answered, "Master, we have worked all night long but have caught nothing. Yet if you say so, I will let down the nets." When they had done this, they caught so many fish that their nets were beginning to break. So they signaled their partners in the other boat to come and help them. And they came and filled both boats, so that they began to sink. But when Simon Peter saw it, he fell down at Jesus' knees …. For he and all who were with him were amazed at the catch of fish. (Lk 5:1–9)

The following is one of the post-resurrection encounters in John's Gospel:

> Just after daybreak, Jesus stood on the beach …. Jesus said to them, "Children, you have no fish, have you?" They answered him, "No." He said to them, "Cast the net to the

right side of the boat, and you will find some." So they cast it, and now they were not able to haul it in because there were so many fish. That disciple whom Jesus loved said to Peter, "It is the Lord!" When Simon Peter heard that it was the Lord, he put on some clothes ... and jumped into the sea. But the other disciples came in the boat, dragging the net full of fish, for they were not far from the land, only about a hundred yards off.

When they had gone ashore, they saw a charcoal fire there, with fish on it, and bread. Jesus said to them, "Bring some of the fish that you have caught." So Simon Peter went aboard and hauled the net ashore, full of large fish, a hundred fifty-three of them; and though there were so many, the net was not torn. (Jn 21:4–11)

To ask whether or not these are memories of two separate events, or whether one of them is somehow inauthentic or which of them was historically the earlier, is the wrong approach. Both texts are authentic. Both texts join together in *equal* witness to the resurrection and yet also interrogate each other and resist any easy, fixed categorization and analysis that would seek to reduce either text to a simple linear narrative structure: the "real" or "historic" order in which things happened. Both texts challenge us to work with them equally to find resonance and, thereby, they also offer us a space in which to explore our own experience of the resurrected Jesus and the "yet-more" of God.

This risk-shaped way of reading, a creative linking of narratives, always works to keep alive textual newness. A risk-shaped way of reading refuses to allow complacency and over-familiarity to compromise our proclamation; it commits us, instead, to thinking outside the box and to bringing playful inquisitiveness

alongside serious respect and reverence for Scripture as we
interpret God's words of life in our generation.

How we might read and interpret the Bible afresh

Those of us familiar with standard Christian liturgical practice
are aware that it is customary to end the reading of Scripture with
a phrase such as, "This is the word of the Lord" or else, "This is
the gospel of the Lord," to which everyone present replies with
something like: "Thanks be to God." *But how is it the word of the
Lord?* Most of us approach Scripture as something "given,"
something whose significance is fundamentally fixed and readily
accessible. The task of preaching and proclamation, of textual
study and scriptural analysis, can then become a matter of gleaning
the meaning from the surface of the text and applying it, like a
patent medicine, to our lives. Even the word we use for a few
verses or paragraphs of Scripture, "passage," suggests superficiality:
a brief sight-seeing trip through the words and phrases and a quick
transaction with the loose change of meaning, like a tourist paying
to catch hurried glimpses of a few key sites. Contrast this with the
word "portion," the normal term in Jewish practice. This word is
more richly redolent of sitting and tasting, of patient rumination,
of taking time for discussion and debate, of asking questions and of
telling stories in reply.

We seem unable to find our way out from under the
deadweight of traditional interpretations and scholarly opinion. We
have lost sight of Scripture as living words and speech that invite
us to risk stepping aside, entering, and engaging with God-in-the-
texts. We no longer allow Jesus' parables to open us to the
unbounded possibilities of the transcendent or to shatter the
matrix we think of as reality in order to become vulnerable before
God and so enable God to allow us to be changed.

We much prefer to make Jesus into the once-for-all rigid

parable of God's Word, rather than seeing him as someone pointing to something bigger. We see this tendency to reduce Jesus in the famous narrative of the encounter on the Emmaus Road. This story, though found in embryo in Mark 16:12–13, becomes an allegory in Luke. In Luke's version, Jesus is depicted as the key to unlocking the interpretive DNA that decodes and explains the "whole meaning" of Hebrew Scripture:

> Then he said to them, "Oh, how foolish you are, and how slow of heart to believe all that the prophets have declared! Was it not necessary that the Messiah should suffer these things and then enter into his glory?" Then beginning with Moses and all the prophets, he interpreted to them the things about himself in all the scriptures. ... They said to each other, "Were not our hearts burning within us while he was talking to us on the road, while he was opening the scriptures to us?" (Lk 24:25–27, 32)

What exactly does "he interpreted to them the things about himself in all the scriptures" mean? The early church certainly wanted to show that Jesus was the Messiah, the fulfillment and completion of Israel's hopes. The "things about himself in all the scriptures" were the interpretations of Hebrew Scripture that were offered in Christian worship: readings of Scripture that put Jesus at the center. Hope, aspiration, and meaning stopped at—and were fixed on—Jesus. And it has been largely so ever since. We no longer have to penetrate the surface, burrow into the text, or go off in search of meaning. The work is done already: Jesus is the answer.

Yet if this Emmaus Road encounter happened as Luke describes it, then Jesus may likely have used his normal subversive style of interpretation and got the disciples to make imaginative connections between texts. He may even have encouraged them to make connections that did not arrive at the easy and predictable equation of Jesus with the fulfillment of messianic prophecy: for such an interpretation positions Jesus *over against* those Jews who failed to recognize him, or "understand him" in that way. He may rather have hoped the disciples would arrive at the discovery of something immensely greater and more creative than this. In fact Jesus may have wanted them to see that the common characteristics of God's touch and action were present both in the Hebrew Scripture and in their own experience of his resurrected self, and that the same trustworthy God was at work for them now as much as in the days of their ancestors.

Was that why their hearts were burning within them, because of their excitement at being drawn and empowered by Jesus to risk engaging with the God of Scripture? A God who does not demand one exclusive reading of meaning and truth set over against and to the detriment of another? Perhaps the disciples' hearts burned because they saw a way of reading that allows the "multi-layeredness" of Scripture to speak in different ways to different people in different contexts. Perhaps the disciples found and claimed for themselves the liberating and transformative power of God at work in their lives as much and as powerfully as Jesus did in his life.

Contrary to what some Christians may think, Scripture is not neutral, inert, or transparent, as much as we might prefer it to be. Scripture cannot be applied "straight from the page." It always requires interpretation and is always and endlessly open to interpretation. Scripture will not be ignored indifferently; it always demands attentiveness. The question for us, as it was for Jesus, the Gospel writers, and the teachers of the early church, is how we are to approach it.

Much further down the Emmaus Road, to the place where it

passes through our own cities and neighborhoods, we are confronted by the same dilemmas. What connections are we able to make with the historic texts of Scripture as we have received them? Do we want "ready-to-wear" answers or will we make our own journey of exciting discovery? How far are we comfortable using what theologians often term a "hermeneutic of suspicion" to question and challenge the traditional interpretations and connections between texts? How might we learn from Jesus to juggle cautious fidelity to long-established understandings with spontaneous and life-giving interpretations and thereby find ourselves re-energized in the process? In particular, how might we use Jesus' insights into the relationship between Scripture and lived experience to help us to re-imagine what feminist theologians (Grey 181) call the "kin-dom" of God and so, somewhere along the way, also find refreshment for the Body of Christ?

Time to think about your own experience

In a time of silence you may now wish to consider your answers to the following questions. If you are with others in a group you may choose to share your responses with them.

- How do you understand prophecy? When Jesus is described as "fulfilling Scripture" what does this mean to you?

- What is Jesus trying to get the Pharisees to see by challenging them about their interpretation of the Law?

- Why does Jesus make outsiders part of the community? Who are the outsiders in your community? What is Jesus asking you to do in relation to them?

- What is the danger with fixed meanings for Scripture?

- How is Scripture the "Word of the Lord" for you? What
  methods do you use for "getting under its skin"? How
  might Jesus' way of handling Scripture help you? What
  might you do if your interpretation of a text differs from
  those of other Christians or church leaders?

Imagining a New "Kindom" Text for the Church

Much like the rich man who built barns for his property in
Jesus' parable but discovers he is about to die (Lk 12:13–21),
contemporary Western society suffers from acute disorientation.
Our comfortable Western understanding of the world has come
increasingly "unstuck." Our safe, one-dimensional, and
unquestioning reading of reality, with its required conformity and
self-centered practices geared to promoting our domination and
authority at the expense of difference, plurality, and the interests
of justice for all, has been brought up sharp. A new world order is
arriving, not by a bad dream, but by the breaking in of a *new* reality
to which we must re-orientate ourselves. We must learn afresh to
flourish and find fullness of life alongside (and no longer over
against or in competition with) the rest of humanity and creation,
or else face our imminent demise.

The need for imagination

God's newness and novelty is breaking in. Jesus' ministry
exemplifies how imagination is at the heart of the proclamation of

the "kingdom-kindom" of God. Indeed, it seems clear that imagination is a theological necessity. For, given our post-modern world of uncertainty and insecurity, it is only by faithfully, *trust*fully, casting the line of our imagination out into the darkness and the unknown toward the hiddenness of God that we can reconnect with the greater reality we all desire.

Imagination is essential if we are to see what human flourishing looks like. Imagination enables us to expand our language and practice and to anticipate the "not-yet" and the "still-more" of God. Imagination allows us to visualize and articulate something of God's alternative reality, where the experience of radical new beginnings is normal and commonplace and faithful to the nature of God revealed in Jesus. Imagination helps us to straddle the "what-is" and the "what-might-be," to birth something new into being and so begin to embody newness in our lives.

The ability to imagine and re-imagine the kingdom of God, as Jesus does repeatedly in the Gospels, is the means by which we (with God's grace) might escape our enthrallment with death and begin to understand our existence in terms of natality and continually fresh beginnings. We can begin to see the world through the lens of resurrection and the re-creative nature of God. Indeed the "kingdom-kindom" of God might stand as a metaphor, a *grace*ful or grace-filled space, in which we are able to open ourselves up to the God who can and might do anything. A space where we can imagine new possibilities, not only for who and what we are and for what new forms of relating there might be, but more fundamentally for how God might be imagined. This is manifestly what Jesus was about.

Imagination and the church

Faithfully imitating the imaginative practice of Jesus also challenges us to reconsider our ways of being church. Many of the church's "foundational texts" (its use of the "one body" metaphor or its self-understanding as "one, holy, catholic, and apostolic," as well as its pastoral practices and disciplines) have their roots in a different age when the pursuit of conformity and the desire for an identity *over against* alternative faiths, ideologies, and life-styles was paramount. Although the historic practice of the church was never uniform or mono-cultural, as it believes, the idea that the church needs to be homogenous may well appear too ideological for today's world where difference and plurality are welcome and valued. Indeed, the very desire for a monolithic, universal form of authority, structure of belief, and an obsession with control and managing heterodoxy may be seen (with hindsight) as contributing to the current plight of the church.

The church has become an institution obsessed with sin and death. It has behaved as though it is the sole arbiter of salvation and has reduced the idea of resurrection life to mean the mere survival of death by more life rather than the unspeakably "life-now-changing" phenomenon that is the witness of the Gospels. The church has muted the good news of the God who gives life to the dead and hindered the experience of radical, energizing amazement.

The image of the earliest Christian community presented in Acts is one that seems alive to its sense of vocation. However much the actual stories and details have been edited, the impression of the church in Acts is that the church is a group filled and empowered by new and vibrant energy. The church witnesses to an utterly changed reality; it needs to create a regime of care that embodies the re-creative love it had seen and touched firsthand in its encounter with the resurrected Jesus.

We need to learn from this story in Acts and re-imagine the church, its categories of belief, and the effects of these beliefs on its pastoral practice. In particular, we must challenge the church's tendency to exclusivity and superiority in relation to other world faiths. We must come to see that the church is not called to embody and manifest all truth and perfection but to be a sign of the kingdom and a source of support, inspiration, and transformation for all. The church is meant to model wholeness and flourishing in the world because it understands that God's creation is still unfinished. Its God-given vocation is to explore and interact with creation's contingency by valuing theological openness, an adventurous spirit of inquiry, imaginative risk-taking, and venturesome loving.

What would today's church feel like if it could stop judging, preaching, and ministering long enough to allow God to break in and speak the words that gave life to the dead Jesus in a faraway garden tomb? (What were these words? Have you ever imagined?) What would the church look like if it were to allow God to open it up enough to regain that re-energized sense of vocation that flows from being aware of the touch of the God who calls into existence things that do not exist? What if the church were to embrace a new humility of vision and a fresh direction to its proclamation and pastoral care?

Is it possible for us to begin to work with God to imagine into existence a new and re-created community of believers? Is it possible to imagine a community for whom belief, care, and openness to God's unbounded potential and gentleness of being form the expression of an embodied practical faith-in-action? Can we imagine a practical, embodied faith-in-action that would not attempt to maintain or enhance social order or the control of the norms and parameters of belief and morality or even scriptural interpretation? Can we imagine a faith-in-action that would concern itself with cultivating maturity and independence, with exploring and nurturing intimacy and justice, and with offering imaginative, inclusive, and transformative pastoral care? Or is this just too much to hope for?

The church's call to witness to the brokenhearted

If the church is called to be anything, it is called to be truly
just and inclusive, imaginative, and re-creative. It is called to give
witness to the essential nature of God. It is called to be an effective
community of hope offering a radical alternative witnessing both to
Jesus' subversive teaching and to his physical brokenness, both of
which lie at the heart of the Christian proclamation.

This need to witness imaginatively to brokenness is especially
critical. Not only because of the obvious necessity to be faithful to
the historical reality of the crucifixion as a permanent reference
point for Christian meaning, but because brokenness—fracture,
disintegration, unraveling, discontinuity, alienation, crisis,
change—is the place where God breaks in and where meaningful
spiritual growth happens. This urgent need to witness to
brokenness is the springboard for an authentic Christian ministry
and effective pastoral practice. By listening attentively to people
and imagining itself into their experience, the church can engage
with brokenness, work with messiness, and stand alongside pain
and suffering. The church can then help individuals sift the chaos
of their lives and identify the pieces and fragments with which God
might begin the work of re-creation. By discerning, naming, and
cooperating with God's re-creative love-in-action the church
might help to birth more complete, mature, and valued selves
better able to explore and live intimacy and justice as embodied
social individuals. In this way it is possible for the church to offer
an imaginative, transformative, and thoroughly practical care and
concern for the world and its diverse communities.

Ten strategies for the church

Consider the story of Moses and Aaron and allow their
experience to play a little in our imaginations. What might it be like
if these men were to return and speak God's truth to today's

religious establishment? Tempted as they might be to rely on harsh words and plagues, they might offer ten strategies (not set in stone but open to ongoing development) that the people of God need in order to confront the vested interest and power ruling our world. How might God use them to create a new text for the church? And what might that new text look like? Cue Moses and let him speak.

1. **Mirror Jesus' ministry of radical equality, justice, and inclusivity.** You cannot be a follower of Jesus and believe that the only thing that matters is your own soul or relationship with God. God demands your involvement in the justice issues of your lifetime. Cease discriminating against those who are unlike you, those who see things differently and who have been made to feel that they are second-class outsiders. God will not tolerate double-dealing with one level of access to resources for you and your sort and a different standard for others.

2. **Do not be afraid to let go of the need for certainty and black-and-white thinking of any kind; it is not of God.** You have come to rely on the need for scientific experts and hard factual knowledge, but real wisdom welcomes plurality, multivalence, and difference. Religious beliefs are not meant to offer unequivocal certainty and are as much working theories as the rest of human knowledge. If accepted uncritically, religious beliefs merely reinforce boundaries and prejudice. Jesus always worked for dialogue and debate instead of stone-throwing.

3. **Be especially careful about the need for certainty as you read Scripture.** In Scripture, as nowhere else, you will find truth through holding together diverse interpretations and different perspectives on the risk-shaped ministry of Jesus.

Be careful that your reading does not lead you to believe that being a Christian gives you preferential access to God at the expense of other people whom you imagine remain somehow less in God's eyes.

4. **Stop assuming that you have to have the stories, texts, and words of Scripture completely tamed and pigeonholed.** Always approach Scripture by assuming that there is much more to be understood beneath the surface. Read Scripture with careful, imaginative attention, expecting to find new things. Being faithful to Scripture does not mean to repeat or believe it literally; being faithful means to look for how the texts trigger questions, responses, and reactions for your world. Look for new connections between the texts and your experience. Never doubt that the re-creative energy of God is waiting in the words of Scripture, for it was written in response to the call to life uttered by the living God. The texts witness to the awesome power of the God who gives life to the dead, so free the texts from the chains of your liturgies and lectionaries and let them loose in the world.

5. **Do not use power the way the world uses power. The power of presidents and rulers, politicians, the military, and big business is not real power.** Do not be seduced by the chance to do something important or glamorous in the eyes of popular opinion. Never cease to look for the demands of God's justice in the world. You will not need to look far. Remember that authority is not something you have over another person or situation; it is the willingness to nurture, not control. If you think otherwise about authority your understanding of God may need revising.

6. **While there are clues to the nature of God in the life and ministry of Jesus, God is ultimately beyond your knowing.** Everything you can say is contingent, a metaphor, and relative. Sometimes you will be unable to say anything at all. Help people to locate their lives within the long story of human evolution, the working of God's universe, and the bigger picture of eternity that enfolds it.

7. **Like Jesus on the cross and his follower Paul of Tarsus, learn to value weakness and failure.** Learn that the darkness was also created by God and is a necessary and normal part of human life. Find time to explore darkness and the meaning of failure and learn how to discern God at work in the silence. Practice humility and saying sorry. Learn that ministry is not about imposing doctrines or morality; it is about loving, so stop judging people.

8. **Try with all your might to rescue people from the deathliness that seeks to consume them.** Model transformative thinking and alternative ways of living. Show people how to find reconciliation and value difference. Offset the total reliance on technology and encourage art and creativity and refute the notion that these are the privilege of trained experts and professionals.

9. **Explore authentic spirituality and prayer based on an unconditional value of every individual and their closeness to the divine.** Challenge the dominant ways of seeing the world. Withstand consumerism with the good news that life and people are of infinite worth just as they are. Resist the insidious pornographic mindset by

a clearer valuing of the human body as a locus of the divine. Promote a discerning need for enchantment by encouraging wonder and care for the environment and the planet. Your track record on both of these is abysmal.

10. **Encourage an imaginative approach in all things.** Imagination is where the human mind meets and mingles with divine inspiration. The church is prophetic when it strives to keep imagination alive. Jesus demonstrated imagination by following the hunch he felt at his baptism. Remember that following your imagination always involves risk, just as it did long ago for Moses and Aaron in Pharaoh's audience room. Real imagination, unlike fantasy, always takes you where you never intended to go. Imagination also demands humility, because it requires you to acknowledge that God is the source of all hope, all possibility, and all potential.

A new text for the church

So here we have it: ten places to begin the business of identifying how the people of God who follow Jesus might identify a way forward. Ten points of entry for discerning how to open ourselves to God's re-creative love and thirst for justice. Ten dynamics for developing an embodied pastoral practice rooted in the scriptural demand to confront the vested interest and ruling powers in our world. Ten ways of demonstrating our commitment to love as Jesus loved, ten sure roads that might lead us to discover what we are most looking for. And ten paths where we will surely encounter risk, challenge, and change. In short, we have a risk-shaped strategy for discipleship.

Time to think about your own experience

In a time of silence you may now wish to consider your answers to the following questions. If you are with others in a group you may choose to share your responses with them.

- Does everyone in your church (have to) believe the same thing and share the same Christian identity? Does "oneness" mean "sameness"? Why or why not?

- When does your church really practice what it preaches? What examples do you have? How is the desire to live out God's thirst for justice a part of the church's ministry and of your own personal witness?

- Walter Brueggemann describes the church as "a place of large dreams." What do you make of this extraordinary statement? How and where is this statement true in your experience? Is your church a place for nurturing the imagination? If not, how could this happen?

- Re-order the ten strategies listed above according to the importance that you think they have.

CHAPTER 8

Piecing Together a Risk-shaped Discipleship

The Western world takes risk and security very seriously. We who live in so-called "developed" nations live in societies that are so preoccupied with the need to identify enemies and anticipate threats that it often seems our entire economy, collective social effort, and our God-given creativity are employed solely to this end.

There is no doubt, of course, that this fear and anxiety are linked to the speed of change in our world. Despite what we might believe about ourselves, our actual understanding of what it means to be human, to respond to our call to live justly and sustainably in the world, and to share the earth's resources equitably has not yet caught up with our obsessive desire to control everything. We have lost touch with the ways to live in the world that most deeply resonate with the fabric of our being. Even the simple act of looking into the night sky and seeing the unmapped vastness of the universe does not give us joy or affinity with creation; we feel dread and paranoia at what might be out there threatening our survival. We cannot put our fearful, anxious minds at rest.

At every level of existence we Westerners have become a nervous and risk-conscious society: one that is averse to the slightest hazard or threat to our security, comfort, or perceived well-being. In previous times, of course, risk (the possibility of mishap, accident, catastrophe, or death) was understood to be part of our routine engagement with the everyday uncertainty of living. But we now assume that all threats and risks must be eliminated as far as humanly possible through scientific expertise and the infallible application of technology. We find the thought of living with any sort of risk intolerable. We are intimidated by the challenges of everyday life and so engage in interminable negotiations about risk. We demand a risk-free existence, which may ultimately prove to be our undoing.

The recent "Risk Commission" of the Royal Society for the encouragement of Arts, Manufactures and Commerce (RSA), in the United Kingdom, reported that our individual ability to assess comparative risk is fading as the world becomes more complex. The Commission found that, as a result, we are being encouraged to abdicate our responsibility for the discernment of risk and give it to public bodies and the scrutiny of experts and systems. This will typically involve a computer somewhere calculating that a postal or zip code suggests a statistically higher risk for the security of a house and property (and a higher likelihood of a claim on a policy and a greater threat to insurers' profits) than the risk of someone living a mile away. Or the unforeseen possibilities arising from traveling abroad must be identified and evaluated before we are allowed to fly. Whatever the scenario, some complex algorithmic formula, created solely by the drive to reduce the cost of risk, legislates what is an acceptable level of risk to the industry, to national security, to society at large, or to individuals.

Given this tendency of risk aversion, it becomes possible to visualize ourselves delegating all potential future human activity, adventure, and development to these soulless methods and so become totally dependent on their ability to plot and navigate hazardous activity on the basis of the minimization of risk and the avoidance of any possible danger or anxiety. Inevitably the human imagination would be reduced to the realm of what is merely financially justifiable and economically viable within the short-term vision and self-serving accountability of governments and transnational corporations with their need to maximize profits. What then for the future of the human spirit?

Risk and the church

These same attitudes towards risk can be seen equally in the church in unwillingness to engage with the perceived riskiness of alternative forms of thinking and action. Witness the increasing preference for closed systems of theological thought and biblical interpretation. Witness the anxiety about engaging in social action and engaging with new understandings of human identity, sexuality, and relationships. In many ways we should not be surprised. The church has always sought to define itself over against social change and has generally adapted belatedly and rather reluctantly. At the start of the twenty-first century the church's theological self-understanding and pastoral practices are speedily atrophying once again. And once again, the church is struggling to be relevant.

Living on the edge: following our ancestors in risk

The Christian faith is oriented toward the future, to the undisclosed end of all things, to the mystery of life after death, to living with the uncertainty of God's ongoing revelation, and to stepping out as pilgrims into the unknown; our faith is also a faith whose members are part of a community of believers that is being continually re-created, a community that is called to work with God's unbounded potential to conceive and birth into existence a world that is forever unfolding. The Christian community is called to walk the "growing edge of things" as a new world of radical justice and openness to change comes into existence.

Like the overwhelming majority of Westerners, we Christians are inveterately anxious and remain eternally hungry for what we feel we lack, yet we have the witness of Abraham and Sarah who, at God's urging, set out into the unknown. Their expedition was dwarfed by the inner journey they made from anxiety to the hope embodied in the arrival of their child and expressed in a mutually creative covenant with God.

We have the witness of Moses who overcame crippling angst and the pain of a tortured and divided identity to confront mighty Pharaoh's deluded notion of his self-sufficiency and authority. Moses discovered an alternative model of power—a fire that burns without consuming—and a God whose passion is for justice, inclusivity, and the freedom and flourishing of all nations. We have Jeremiah's witness to the durability of the covenant and the trustworthiness of God. God's trust was both revealed and concealed within the hardships, trials, and contingencies of the chaos and upheaval of his day. We have Isaiah's witness. Isaiah discovered the treasures in the darkness, the "yet-more" of God. From Isaiah we learn that we can get on the inside of God's unconditional love, and that if we heed the venturesome call to enter God's love, we will find that this love is the touchstone for the in-breaking of radical newness, transformative power, and flourishing.

Risk-taking is nowhere better illustrated than in the person of Jesus. Risk came naturally to Jesus. His faith, his practical wisdom-in-action, was thoroughly risk-shaped. And if we wish to call ourselves Christian, we have no choice but to imitate him. Jesus heeded the sense of possibility he experienced at his baptism. His response to the Spirit's call to enter the terrible dark night of the desert to face his inner demons and doubts brought about a transformation—and an empowerment—that began his extraordinary ministry and fulfilled his destiny. Time and again he took risks and invited others to do the same until, faced with the supreme test, he took on even death itself—not knowing the outcome, but fully convinced that what he had discovered on the inside of his relationship with God was sufficiently trustworthy.

This task of following hunches and discerning possibilities is one that we need to rediscover. For it will enable us to open ourselves to the "yet-more" of God and create a trustworthy spirituality of engagement with anxiety and change, and teach us to articulate a radical prophetic message for our time.

Change is part of life

We may consider that an openness to risk is extraordinarily difficult to achieve, but only if we forget something very obvious about life: change is a profoundly normal thing. Daily we experience that life is in flux. Creation constantly moves forward, from new moment to new moment, from new birth to new birth, and we are carried along with creation out into the unknown. Despite this experience of life, we often find ourselves looking backwards, trying to root ourselves to the spot and cling to the old—reluctant in the extreme to engage with the exhilarating business of change.

What can help us discover that God inhabits change, contingency, and provisionality as readily as we have understood God's self-revelation to be historic, complete, and unchanging?

What might it take for us to come to see change as a virtuous cycle of newness and flourishing instead of a vicious cycle of decay and futility? What might motivate us to let go of our anxiety about change and risk plunging down into the deep waters of God's shimmering, re-creative darkness?

People change only if they can be persuaded by some desire from within or beyond themselves. A discipleship that embraces change, one committed to inhabiting a changing world and to finding God within change, responds to the lure, to the scent or voice of the divine, as it calls us to open ourselves to ongoing re-creation. Such a disciple is open to fresh perspectives, adopts a critical questioning approach, and is willing to think outside the box. Such a disciple is willing to walk the boundaries of experience and knowledge and to work with God to help usher in what lies beyond the horizon.

This book began with a question. Is it possible to develop a framework for discerning and exploring the art of spiritual risk-taking that encourages people to engage with their fears about change? The biblical evidence we have examined provides potent examples to reflect upon during our journey. This evidence offers us tools to use in creating a risk-shaped discipleship, a discipleship that will enable us to embody our faith within the disciplines and practices of everyday human living. What are these tools?

- **Unlearning in the darkness outside of the box**
  Darkness, mystery, discomfort, and unknowing will be the watchwords of our discipleship. We will rediscover that the darkness is welcoming and fundamental to our existence as the fecund source of newness and re-creation. We will accept that our security is not vested in fixed theological, moral, or intellectual certainties and we will need to relinquish control of ideas. We will reject our dependency on risk-free revelation and re-learn how to be comfortable with mystery, partial knowledge, and unfolding wisdom.

- **Living on the boundaries**
  We will familiarize ourselves with the twilight zones and liminal places of human experience and discover the pathways that allow us to cross back and forth over the boundary between what is safe and secure and what is perilous and risk-filled, between what-is and what-is-yet-to-be. Being a boundary walker and go-between—a voyager across frontiers—requires an openness to otherness and to differences, an ability to learn to understand and express ourselves in an unfamiliar

language, and a capacity to cope with what is strange and
novel, to cope with what reduces us to silence.

- **Learning how to play again**
  As anyone knows who has tried to speak in a new
  language and then finds himself or herself using strange
  gestures and a new body language, exploring new places
  provides us with the opportunity to become different
  people. Inhabiting a different world will encourage us to
  learn an attitude of playfulness with which to uncover
  different aspects of ourselves and the universe around us.
  We will learn how to laugh at ourselves and with others
  and how to improvise new ways of being. Play will help us
  satisfy our need to get in touch with the deepest of our
  desires—the desire for connection, enchantment, and
  delight at being alive.

- **Imagining newness into being**
  If we refuse to be armchair theological travelers any longer,
  dependent on the experience of others, if we dare
  ourselves to set out on our own adventures, we will
  discover that what we bring back and share effectively
  helps to re-imagine the status quo. Embracing our God-
  given imagination will enable us to see through God's eyes
  and allow us to overcome the deep-seated competitiveness
  that drives our anxiety. It is our imagination, nurtured and
  exercised through creative activity and prayer that will
  help us cooperate with God's re-creative action.

- **Disciplining ourselves to discern**
  While using our imagination is critical we will need a
  commitment to the individual and collective discipline of
  prayerful and prophetic discernment about the gifts and

insights we receive. We will learn to measure ourselves and our actions against the "kindom ethic" by placing mutual accountability at the center and as the base criterion for all our actions. Whatever is granted to us will be for the building up of the whole community, for the flourishing of all people, and for the planet itself.

- **Living in the present moment**
  If we measure our actions, we will find ourselves better able to live in the present moment. We will not focus on satisfying just our own appetites ("eating and drinking, for tomorrow we die" or living carelessly without appreciation for the gift of life) but on embodying Jesus' often ignored teaching about lilies of the field and birds of the air (Mt 6:25–34; Lk 12:22–31).

  We will learn to delight in contingency, in the ever-changing rhythms of life, in the uncertainties of our existence and to become proficient in improvising our responses to newness and novelty as it emerges. This openness will transform the way we make our home in the universe. We will teach our children to dance with the creative improvisation of life itself.

- **Traveling as a covenant people**
  The consistent witness of Scripture is that God is not-like-other-gods. We are called to inhabit the world by following the example of the fire that burns without destroying the bush. We will discover how to be ourselves (the people God called us to be) without living at the expense of other people. We will not only believe in, but will act out of God's trustworthy call to live based on the covenant God has made with each of us.

This covenant, constantly reaffirmed in God's developing relationship with us, is still as dynamic and fruitful today as it was in the past. The covenant functions as the default position between God and us and as the sign of God's desire for mutuality with all people. It also allows us to engage with contingency and anticipate change while still working with the continuous and consistent unfolding of God's re-creative love.

By seeking to discern the mutuality of the covenant—from moment to moment and from place to place—we might just be persuaded to let go of our urge to selfish competitiveness. It is by recognizing and naming the creative outworking of God's venturesome love that we might dare ourselves to trust a newfound instinct for cooperation and synergy with God, revealed unfailingly in the biblical stories of the functional proficiency of the covenant in action. This covenant demands that we name injustice wherever it is found and ally ourselves with the persecuted. We will work ceaselessly to create a community of kinship, interconnectedness, and celebration.

Celebration—because it's *worship!*

If the covenant has any value at all today and, more to the point, if it is worth staking our lives on and risking our souls, then the church will see itself in a different light. The church will be able to make a fresh commitment to its original purpose: the nurturing of a true "resurrection life" that embodies God's covenant and enables and promotes flourishing in the world. The church will become a place where a new matrix is revealed and people can experience re-creation in their own bodies, in their relationships, and in their lives.

If worship has any value in terms of articulating gratitude and delight in God's gratuitous love for creation, then the church will embody a heightened sense of spiritual companionship and create a more genuine and practical ministry of hospitality—one that we might worthily call a discipline of feasting, celebration, and worship.

A new matrix is revealed

And here we have come to the end of our deliberations. The call of God has been heard. The time to act is upon us. Like Abraham and Sarah, like Moses, like Jeremiah and Isaiah, and like Jesus, we have already set off toward the future. Even now we are preparing to bring to birth whatever is given us to be and to do. Alone or in the company of others, we must now go out and claim the risk-shaped discipleship that is our own unique gift for the world.

Time to think about your own experience

In a time of silence you may now wish to consider your answers to the following questions. If you are with others in a group you may choose to share your responses with them.

- What are we called to unlearn in the darkness?

- What boundaries are we called to cross?

- Why do we need to learn to play again?

- What do we need to do to imagine newness for our church?

- Where can we go to acquire the discipline of discernment?

- What will help us begin to live in the present moment?

- Whom can we invite to travel with us as a covenant people?

- Whom must we invite to celebrate with us in order to make it worship?

- Where do we go from here to work for the flourishing of our world?

Works Cited

Alison, James. *On Being Liked*. London: DLT, 2003.

Anselm, Saint. *Proslogium*. Christian Classic Ethereal Library:
www.ccel.org/ccel/schaff/anf01.ix.vii.xviii.html.

Arendt, Hannah. *The Human Condition, Second Edition*. Chicago:
University of Chicago Press, 1998. © 1958 by the University of
Chicago. All rights reserved.

Athanasius. *On the Incarnation*. Christian Classic Ethereal Library:
www.ccel.org.

Biddington, Terry. "Why on Earth is Gender still such an Issue?"
Franciscan (May 2005).

Bowie, Fiona, ed. *Beguine Spirituality: An Anthology*. London:
SPCK, 1989.

Brock, Rita Nakashima. *Journeys by Heart: A Christology of Erotic
Power*. Eugene, OR: Wipf & Stock, 2008.

Brueggemann, Walter. *Mandate to Difference: An Invitation to the
Contemporary Church*. Louisville, KY: Westminster John Knox
Press, 2007.

Clement of Alexandria. *Stromata*. New Advent:
www.newadvent.org.

Dionysius the Areopagite. *Mystical Theology*. Christian Classic
Ethereal Library: www.ccel.org.

Grey, Mary C. *Sacred Longings: Ecofeminist Theology and Globalisation*. London: SCM Press, 2003.

Hadewijch: The Complete Works. London: SPCK, 1980.

Hull, John. *In the Beginning There Was Darkness*. London: SCM Press, 2001.

Irenaeus. *Against Heresies, Book V.* Christian Classic Ethereal Library: www.ccel.org/ccel/schaff/anf01.ix.vii.xviii.html

Johnson, Gerry and Kevan Scholes. *Exploring Corporate Strategy*. London: Prentice Hall Europe, 1999.

Leech, Kenneth. *Soul Friend: A Study of Spirituality*. London: Sheldon Press, 1977.

Lewin, Kurt. *Field theory in social science; selected theoretical papers*. New York: Harper & Row, 1951.

Newman, Barbara. *Sister of Wisdom: St. Hildegard's Theology of the Feminine*. Berkeley: University of California Press, 1987.

Pfeiffer, Franz. *Meister Eckhart*. London: John M Watkins, 1956.

RSA Risk Commission: www.thersa.org/projects/past-projects/risk-commission.

Scarry, Elaine. *The Body in Pain: The Making and Unmaking of the World*. New York: Oxford University Press, 1985.

Sheldrake, Philip. *Spirituality and History: Questions of Interpretation and Method*. London: SPCK, 1991.

Tauler, Johannes. *Sermons (CWS)*. New York: Paulist Press, 1985.

Welch, Sharon. *A Feminist Ethic of Risk.* Minneapolis: Augsburg Fortress, 2000.

Williams, Rowan. "The Authority of the Church." *Modern Believing* 46, no. 1 (Jan. 2005): 16-28. Liverpool: Modern Churchpeople's Union.